The Lucayan Story

The Indigenous People of The Bahamas & Turks and Caicos Islands

Scholastic Edition

Tellis A. Bethel

Copyrights

The Lucayan Story The Indigenous People of The Bahamas and the Turks and Caicos Islands Scholastic Edition. All Rights Reserved. Copyright © 2016 Tellis A. Bethel

ISBN-13: 978-1537372150

ISBN-10: 1537372157

All images courtesy of Wikipedia, unless otherwise stated.

All word definitions are from the Merriam-Webster online dictionary (www.merriam-webster.com) unless otherwise stated.

Edited by: The Manuscript Groomer

This book may not be reproduced, transmitted, or stored in whole or part by any means, including graphic, electronic, or mechanical without the express written consent of the author except in the case of brief quotations embodied in critical articles and reviews.

Dedication

To the next generation of Bahamians:

Seeds of greatness are small things from which great things grow. We should therefore never despise the day of small beginnings as the great nations of the modern Americas exist today because of a tiny seed we call The Bahamas and the Turks and Caicos Islands, otherwise known as the Lucayan archipelago.

On 12th October 1492, Christopher Columbus made his 'accidental' landfall on the shores of these islands. This historic event made these tiny islands the 'birthplace' of the modern Americas or a type of 'motherland' for the entire Western Hemisphere. Consequently, the nations of the modern Americas that exist today came out of the 'geographical womb' of The Bahamas and the Turks and the Caicos Islands.

Mothers are leaders in their own right; they influence their offspring with vision for a better world; integrity for the long term, sustainable development of that world; and purpose for solving problems and meeting the needs of others in that world.

By virtue of their shared heritage, Bahamians and Turks and Caicos Islanders were destined to be leaders who influence others to do their part to make the world a better place. However, the fulfilling of this calling will require the ongoing development of skills and character, the overcoming of challenges, and the making of the changes necessary for a better world.

Ironically, an underlying lesson to be discovered along the path to success in life is revealed through the legacy of the Lucayans--the first known inhabitants of these islands. In telling their story, this book reveals that making the world a better place requires each generation to learn from the mistakes of past and to improve on the positive accomplishments of others while creating success stories of their own.

Such is the call of the next generation of Bahamians in doing their part to make the world a better place in light of the Lucayan story.

Acknowledgements

This work would not have been possible without the loving support of my wonderful wife, Teri, and much encouragement from our two sons, Tellis (Jr.) and Tate. I love and appreciate you all.

List of Illustrations

Fig. 1: Treasure Cay Beach, Abaco, Bahamas

Fig. 2: Tongue of the Ocean

Fig. 3: The Lucayan Archipelago

Fig. 4: Map of The Turks and Caicos Islands

Fig. 5: Map of The Bahamas

Fig. 6: The Bahamas & the Caribbean Map

Fig. 7: 1732 Herman Moll Map of the West Indies and Caribbean

Fig. 8: Map of Islas Lucayas, Ò de Los Lucayos

Fig. 9: The Florida Straits with a Part of the Great Bahama Bank

Fig. 10: Native Carib Indian

Fig. 11: Islands occupied by Lucayans, Tainos & Caribs

Fig.12: Lucayan Indians

Fig.13: Duho—A Ceremonial Chair

Fig.14: Lucayan Dugout Canoe at The Bahamas Historical Society and Museum

Fig. 15: Replica of a Lucayan House, Leon Levy Native Plant Preserve, Eleuthera, Bahamas.

Fig. 16: Bering Land Bridge (Beringia)

Fig. 17: Columbus' Initial Voyage to the New World

Fig. 18: Columbus' Statue Government House, Nassau Bahamas

Fig. 19: Christopher Columbus' First Voyage to the Americas

Fig. 20: Norseman Leif Erikson

Fig. 21: Chinese Admiral Zhen He

Fig. 22: Waldseemüller Map of 1507 showing America as being separate from Asia

Fig. 23: San Salvador Island

Fig. 24: Monument presented by Spain, Landfall Park, San Salvador Island

Fig. 25: Forms of European Torture

Fig. 26: Black Seminoles

Fig. 27: Conquistador Ponce de León Meets Puerto Rican Tainos

Fig. 28: Captain Woodes Rogers

Fig. 29: The Lucayan Sea

Contents

Dedication i
Acknowledgements iii
List of Illustrations iv
Message from Tellis A. Bethel viii
Preface 1
Introduction 3
Excerpt from the Preamble to The Commonwealth of The Bahamas' Constitution 6
Ch. 1 ~ A Story to Tell 7
Ch. 2 ~ The Bahamas & the Turks and Caicos Islands 10
Ch. 3 ~ What's in a Name? 18
Ch. 4 ~ How The Bahamas Got its Name 21
Ch. 5 ~ Lucayan Ancestry 30
Ch. 6 ~ The Lucayan People 37
Ch. 7 ~ Populating the Americas 43
Ch. 8 ~ Old World Meets New World 47
Ch. 9 ~ Other New World Explorers 52
Ch. 10 ~ San Salvador Island 56
Ch. 11 ~ A Quest for Gold 61
Ch. 12 ~ Lucayan Demise 65
Ch. 13 ~ The Black Seminoles 71
Ch. 14 ~ Gold Rush of the Americas 74
Ch. 15 ~ Tracing Lucayan Roots 79
Ch. 16 ~ The Lucayan Legacy 81
Ch. 17 ~ The Lucayan Sea 87

Ch. 18 ~ How the Oceans of the Americas got their Names 94
Ch. 19 ~ Ambassadors of Peace 97
Ch. 20 ~ Discovery Day 104
Appendix ~ Lucayan and Taino Timelines 107
Bibliography 113
Author's Contact 120

Message from Tellis A. Bethel

When we fail to claim our heritage, others will claim it for us.

A 'heritage' is something handed down to a nation or a people. It includes aspects of their history, geography and culture that contain clues for long term success. *The Lucayan Story—The Indigenous People of The Bahamas & the Turks and Caicos Islands* rediscovers the rich heritage shared by The Bahamas and the Turks and Caicos Islands and the waters that surround them to reveal secrets to fulfilling their purpose and destiny.

For the purpose of this book, The Bahamas and the Turks and Caicos Islands are referred to as the 'Lucayan Islands' or the 'Lucayan archipelago,' because they belong to the same chain of islands that was originally inhabited by the indigenous Lucayan people. These terms are generally used by scholars and researchers when referring to the entire island chain.[1] Also in this book, the term 'Bahama chain' refers to The Bahamas only.

In reading the Lucayan Story, it is important to note that the early history of The Bahamas and the Turks and Caicos

Islands tells the story of tragedy and trauma caused by humanity's quest for a better world through the life of the Lucayan people. Ironically, these islands eventually became the geographical 'birthplace of the modern Americas,' which resulted in the demise of the Lucayans.

Additionally, this 'unintended' consequence of history reveals a leadership role that modern-day inhabitants of these islands were destined to play. Furthermore, it uncovers a culture that Bahamians and Turks and Caicos Islanders were meant to display as 'ambassadors of peace.'

The Lucayan Story therefore sheds light on secrets to long term success of modern-day inhabitants of these islands—secrets found within the legacy of the Lucayan people and the heritage they left behind.

The Lucayan Story

Preface

Humanity's age-old quest for a better life has led to profound[1] events taking place within these Lucayan Islands that have changed the course of world destiny. The culmination[2] of the eastward trek of ancient civilization out of Asia; the first landfall of the Italian navigator, Christopher Columbus, in the New World; and the birthing of the modern Americas are just a few examples of world-changing events that have occurred in and around the pristine waters of The Bahamas and the Turks and Caicos Islands.

Now at a crossroad in history, the modern-day inheritors[3] of The Bahamas and the Turks and Caicos Islands recently completed their first 40 years of political and social change (on 10 July 2014) after The Bahamas received its independence from Great Britain on 10 July, 1973. Consequently, both island groups are entering a second 40 year period since this change took place. It is therefore highly likely that the political and administrative leaders of these islands who were present at the beginning of the first

---

[1] Profound: having or showing great knowledge or understanding.
[2] Culmination: the end or final result of something.
[3] Inherit: to receive (money, property, etc.) from someone when that person dies. (An inheritor is someone who receives the money, property, etc.).

40 years will not be around by the end of the next 40 years in 2053.

With the world in an unpredictable state of social unrest and instability, the year 2014 marked the threshold[4] of a new era that can become a defining moment for the people of these islands and the Americas, if they were to rediscover and unearth the rich historical significance of world-changing events that shaped history on their shores centuries ago.

The Lucayan Story—The Indigenous People of The Bahamas and Turks and Caicos Islands is a tribute to the life and legacy[5] of the original inhabitants of The Bahamas and the Turks and Caicos Islands. The Lucayan Story sheds new light on the origins of the modern Americas through the heritage and legacy of these islands.

This eye-opening story begins with an ancient migration and concludes with the settling of these Lucayan islands, and the subsequent 'rebirth' of the New World. More importantly, this book uncovers an identity, purpose, and a destiny for the modern-day inhabitants of these islands, the millions of people who visit their shores, and the peoples of the wider Americas.

---

[4] Threshold: the point or level at which something begins or changes.
[5] Legacy: something that happened in the past or that comes from someone in the past.

Introduction

The pristine waters that surround The Bahamas and the Turks and Caicos Islands, though renowned for their virginal beauty, played much more than an aesthetic (or needless) role in the shaping of the New World during the early period of the modern Americas. The geographical setting of these turquoise waters actually propelled these islands into historical significance as a maritime crossroad that resulted in the permanent reuniting of world civilizations and the unfolding saga of the modern Americas.

Fig. 1: Treasure Cay Beach, Abaco, Bahamas

Today, these tranquil waters belie[6] their turbulent[7] and tragic history; yet despite a marred[8] past, now speak of an identity and a purpose for a people, who by historical accounts were actually destined to become ambassadors of peace in light of a tragic genocide.[9]

Sadly, the Lucayan chain of islands was unmercifully stripped of its original inhabitants, the peaceful Lucayans. These indigenous inhabiters of the land came to this island-paradise in search of a better life, but their quest was met by seize and capture by European colonizers who forced them to work as slaves in the larger northern Caribbean Islands—a region also known as the Greater Antilles. Within a generation of European arrival in the Americas in 1492, the peace-loving Lucayans had been completely extinguished as a people group.

In light of the Lucayan demise, this book uncovers an inherent[10] responsibility bestowed upon today's inhabitants of these islands, as well as their visitors, and the peoples of the wider Americas, to make a personal investment toward making the world a more peaceful place. Evidence of this far-reaching calling can be found throughout the history of The Bahamas and the Turks and Caicos Islands.

Interestingly, the waters of The Bahamas and the Turks and Caicos Islands symbolize the life and legacy of the Lucayans, as well as the rich heritage of the islands they

---

[6] Belie: to give a false idea of (something).
[7] Turbulent: full of confusion, violence, or disorder: not stable or steady.
[8] Mar: to ruin the beauty or perfection of (something): to hurt or damage the good condition of (something).
[9] Genocide: the deliberate killing of people who belong to a particular racial, political, or cultural group.
[10] Inherent: belonging to the basic nature of someone or something.

once inhabited. These unnamed waters are therefore historically rooted in the unfolding of the modern Americas, and are a symbolic reminder to the peoples of these islands and the wider Americas of the inherent[11] calling that was bestowed upon them as a result of the demise of their original inhabitants.

---

[11] Inherent: Belonging by nature.

Excerpt from the Preamble to The Commonwealth of The Bahamas' Constitution

'Whereas four hundred and eighty-one years ago the rediscovery of this Family of Islands, Rocks and Cays heralded the rebirth of the New World....'[2]

Ch. 1 ~ A Story to Tell

Every year millions of visitors make their way throughout the more than 700 islands and cays of The Bahamas and the Turks and Caicos Islands in their quest for paradise. Approximately half of all visitors stay in hotels while the remainder travels to these shores aboard cruise ships. Upon arrival, travelers blissfully explore the natural wonders of this tropical paradise while enjoying a myriad of waterborne activities in a world of peace and rest.

Unbeknownst[12] to the casual visitor, the idyllic[13] islands of The Bahamas and the Turks and Caicos Islands have a profound story to tell. Coincidentally, the Lucayan chain appears to have been aptly[14] furnished by nature to tell this intriguing story. In the midst of this tropical chain of islands near the western border of the North Atlantic Ocean is the Tongue of the Ocean. Equal in depth to the Grand Canyon of Arizona,[3] this deep underwater trench with its tongue-like shape bears witness to the rich history and rare heritage of these lands, which hosted the dramatic, historic events that led to the unfolding of the modern Americas.

---

[12] Unbeknownst: happening or existing without the knowledge of someone specified.
[13] Idyllic: very peaceful, happy, and enjoyable.
[14] Apt: appropriate or suitable.

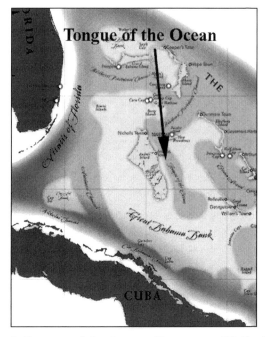

Fig. 2: Tongue of the Ocean (Courtesy of T. Bethel)

The Tongue of the Ocean now bears testimony to the plight[15] and legacy of the indigenous Lucayans, who arrived on these shores in dugout canoes, and whose story dates back to the ancient times of Africa, Europe and Asia. Interestingly, The Bahamas has been listed in the Guinness Book of World Records for having the world's longest serving newspaper editor in the person of Sir Étienne Dupuch (now deceased) of the Nassau Tribune [4]. This record-setting coincidence gives the impression that the story of the Lucayans' quest for peace and knowledge of its underlying significance was meant to last.

---

[15] Plight: an unfortunate, difficult, or precarious situation.

The Lucayan Story

Though relatively unimpressive in size, these islands possess a profound history that matches the depths of their surrounding seas. Despite their idyllic nature, The Bahamas and Turks and Caicos Islands (or the Lucayan Islands) have seen more than their fair share of turmoil over the centuries. Yet, through a series of unintended historic events, these tiny islands have reshaped the destiny of the Americas and the world.

With this level of interest from visitors who frequent the islands each year, along with the rich history, heritage and legacy of these islands, it seems only fitting to dedicate a portion of this picturesque paradise to the memory of the life and plight of the original inhabitants of The Bahamas and the Turks and Caicos Islands.

Questions

1. How many islands make up The Bahamas and the Turks and Caicos Islands?

2. Where is the Tongue of the Ocean geographically located?

3. How deep is the Tongue of the Ocean?

Ch. 2 ~ The Bahamas & the Turks and Caicos Islands

The Bahamas and the Turks and Caicos Islands collectively make up the Lucayan chain of islands. Also known as the Lucayan archipelago, this chain of islands lies near the western boundary of the North Atlantic Ocean, approximately 50 miles (80 km) east of South Florida on the southeast coast of the United States of America.[5] Though inhabited by the Lucayans, the islands were claimed by the Spanish Crown after Christopher Columbus made his first landfall in the Americas on their shores.

The islands extend over 500 miles (800 km) in a southeasterly direction from 50 miles (80 km) off the east coast of Florida to within 15 miles (24 km) of the northern coast of the Republic of Cuba and within 90 miles (144 km) of the northern coast of the island of Hispañiola (the Republic of Haiti and the Dominican Republic).

Today, the Lucayan chain is divided into two groups of islands, The Bahamas and the Turks and Caicos Islands. The Bahamas (or the Bahama chain) comprises the much larger group that runs the full length of the chain, which slants in a northwest to southeast direction. The smaller group of islands, the Turks and Caicos Islands, is located at the southeastern end of the Lucayan chain.

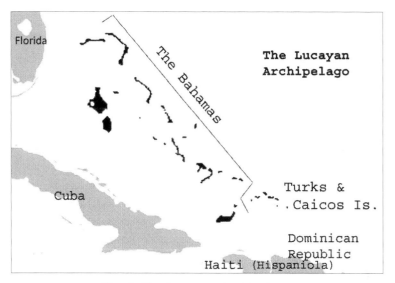

Fig. 3: The Lucayan Archipelago

The name, 'Turks' is believed by some to have been derived from an indigenous cactus plant called the 'Turks Head' (melocactus communis)[6], which has a red top that looks like a fez[7] (a conical red hat worn by people from Turkey). The name, 'Caicos' is from a Lucayan name said to mean 'outer' or 'far away island.'[8] The name Caicos is also said to mean 'string of islands.'[9]

The Bahamas occupies more than 90 percent of the Lucayan chain's landmass with 5,340 square miles (13,940 sq. km) of land. The Turks and Caicos Islands' combined landmass is up to 366 square miles (948 sq. km). The Bahamas' population in 2010 was 350,000[10] in number, approximately ten times the population of the Turks and Caicos Islands, which had some 35,000 people during the same year.[11]

Following the Lucayan genocide, the Lucayan chain of islands was abandoned for over a century. The distinction between The Bahamas and the Turks and Caicos Islands came about after the islands were settled at separate times by English settlers from Bermuda. The Bahamas was reclaimed by the British in 1629, having been granted to English Attorney General Sir Robert Heath.[12]

However, no attempt was made to settle these islands until the arrival of English settlers from Bermuda in 1648 under the leadership of Captain William Sayle. Captain Sayle, a two-time governor of Bermuda, along with seventy settlers from Bermuda, made landfall on an island in the central Bahamas, which they named 'Eleutheria'.

This island was named after the Company of Eleutherian Adventurers that was formed in England for the expedition.[13] The name, Eleutheria (now spelled Eleuthera), comes from the Greek word for 'freedom.' The original Lucayan name for this island was Segatoo.[14] Prior to being resettled in 1666 for the first time since the Lucayans, New Providence Island—the island of The Bahamas' capital city, Nassau—was once named, Sayles Island.[15]

Approximately 30 years after The Bahamas was settled, the Turks and Caicos Islands were also settled by people from Bermuda from as early as 1678.[16] The British, however, did not formally claim the Turks and Caicos Islands until 1764.[17] As the smaller of the two British colonies, the Turks and Caicos Islands came under the jurisdiction of the Bahama colony on several occasions with the initial period beginning in 1766 and ending in 1848—a period of over 80 years.[18]

The Bahamas again exercised jurisdiction over the Turks and Caicos Islands from 1962 to 1973 after Jamaica became independent in 1962.[19] On July 10, 1973, The Bahamas gained its independence from Great Britain. As a result, the Turks and Caicos Islands were separated from

The Bahamas, and the post of administrator on that colony was elevated to governor.

Prior to this, however, Turks and Caicos Islanders began migrating to The Bahamas in search of employment[20] from as early as the 1890s.[21] Today, the Turks and Caicos Islands remain a British Overseas Territory. Nevertheless, The Bahamas and the Turks and Caicos Islands have shared a common history, heritage and legacy as a result of being a part of the same island chain.[22]

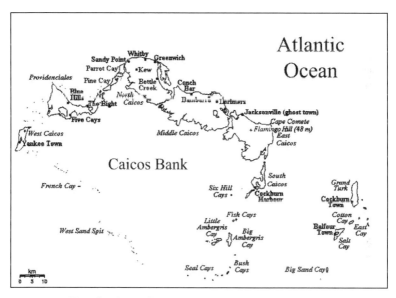

Fig. 4: Map of The Turks and Caicos Islands

Geopolitically[16], the Lucayan chain is often described as being a part of the Caribbean. Geographically, however, the Lucayan chain is separated from the rest of the Caribbean

---

[16] Geopolitically: the political and geographic parts of something.

Islands and nations.[23] The Caribbean chain of islands is divided into two main groups of islands, the Greater Antilles and the Lesser Antilles. The Greater Antilles are the much larger islands (with the exception of the Cayman Islands) in the north of the chain, which include Puerto Rico, Hispañiola, Cuba, and Jamaica.

The Lesser Antilles are the remaining islands, which are also divided into two sub-groups, the Leeward Islands that form the northern half of this sub-group, and the Windward Islands that form the southern half. The southern end of the Windward Islands, which is the Republic of Trinidad and Tobago, lies just a few miles off the northern coast of Venezuela. Unlike the Caribbean Islands and nations, the Lucayan chain of islands does not border the Caribbean Sea.[24]

The Lucayan archipelago is separated from the Caribbean Islands (also known as the Caribbean archipelago) and the Caribbean Sea by a deep marine channel known as the Old Bahama Channel. The Old Bahama Channel exists between the southern boundary of the Bahama chain and the northern Caribbean Islands of Cuba and Hispañiola.

Today, the Old Bahama Channel is a major passageway for cruise ships, as well as other commercial vessels traveling between the American continents. Although the Lucayan chain is not a part of the Caribbean chain of islands, the proximity of The Bahamas and the Turks and Caicos Islands to the Caribbean makes the Lucayan archipelago a part of the Caribbean region.[25]

The Lucayan Story

Fig. 5: Map of The Bahamas

Bermuda is a British Overseas Territory in the North Atlantic Ocean from where the original settlers of The Bahamas and the Turks and Caicos Islands came. It is approximately 769 miles southeast of New York or 900 miles northeast of The Bahamas. Bermuda is therefore not a part of the Lucayan or Caribbean chain of islands; nevertheless, it is characterized as part of the Americas. Although The Bahamas, the Turks and Caicos Islands, and Bermuda are geographically separated from the Caribbean chain, they share a common heritage as being a part of the British West Indies.

The British West Indies is made up of those islands that were once a part of the British Empire. Together, The

Bahamas, the Turks and Caicos Islands, and Bermuda form the northern sector of the British West Indies. Caribbean Islands that are a part of the British West Indies include Antigua and Barbuda, Barbados, Dominica, Cayman Islands (a British Overseas Territory), Jamaica, St. Kitts and Nevis, St. Lucia, St. Vincent and the Grenadines, and Trinidad and Tobago. Guyana in South America and Belize in Central America are also a part of the British West Indies.

Fig. 6: The Bahamas & the Caribbean Map

Questions

1. Where is the Lucayan archipelago located?

2. What country/territory makes up the Lucayan archipelago?

3. How did the Turks and Caicos Islands get its name?

4. Are The Bahamas and the Turks and Caicos Islands a part of the Caribbean Islands?

5. What is the West Indies and where is it located?

Ch. 3 ~ What's in a Name?

From as early as the 1500s,[26] the Spanish referred to the islands of the Lucayan chain as 'Las Islas de Los Lucayos.'[27] (The name 'Lucayas' was also used as seen in Fig. 7). The Dominican Friar Bartolomé de Las Casas had made reference to the 'Lucayos' in his book, La Historia de las Indias (The history of the Indies)[28] —a work he completed in the mid-1500s. Las Casas was a historian and a theologian[29] from Spain who personally witnessed the horrific treatment of the native Tainos of Hispañiola and Cuba, who were ancestors of the Lucayans, during the early years of Spanish colonization of the Americas. As a result of his unyielding efforts to protect the Taino people, Las Casas became known as the 'Defender of the Indians.'[30] Las Casas died in 1566.

The name 'Lucayan' is the English form of the Spanish name, Lucayos.[31] Some scholars suggest that the name Lucayos[32] originated from the Taino words, Lukku Cairi[33] (also spelled Lukku Kairi)[34] or the Arawakan words 'Lukkunu Kairi.'[35] These names are said to mean, 'Island People.' (Cairi or Kairi means Island, and Lukkunu or Lukku means People or Man).[36] 'Lucairi' is another word that means 'Island People.'[37]

Research by Julian Granberry and Gary Vescelius (now deceased) suggests that the modern-day name for The Bahamas came from the Lucayan word, 'Bahama.'[38] This name is purported to mean 'Large Upper Middle Land.'[39] From the early 1500s, an island in the northwestern Bahamas carried the name, Bahama, as shown on a map[40] published in Turin, Italy in 1523.[41] Today, the name of that island is Grand Bahama Island.

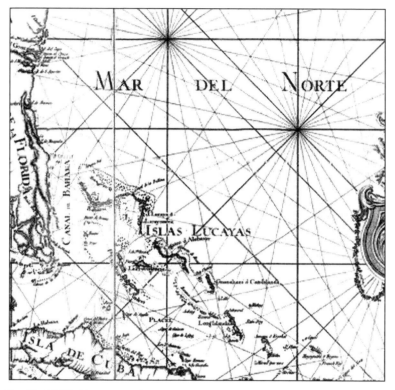

Fig. 7: 1732 Herman Moll Map of the West Indies and Caribbean

By 1670, the name 'Lucayos' along with name 'Bahama' was used to identify all the islands of the Lucayan archipelago as indicated in a Royal Grant to the Lords Proprietors at the time.[42] Some historians and scholars further suggest that the name Bahamas was derived from the Spanish word, 'bajamar' (pronounced, baha mar),[43] which actually means 'shallow sea' or 'low tide.'[44] In more modern Spanish-to-English dictionaries, the Spanish word for 'shallow sea' is spelt 'bajamar.'[45]

Coincidentally, 'the largest single-phase resort development in the history of the Caribbean and the only one of its kind in the Western Hemisphere' to be constructed is using a variation of the name, 'Bahama;' the resort's name is 'Baha Mar.'[46] Original plans for the development include four hotels, including Baha Mar Casino & Hotel with 2,200 rooms, 284 private residences, a 100,000-square-foot (9,300 m2) casino, a 30,000-square-foot (2,800 m2) spa, and a golf course designed by Jack Nicklaus.[47]

Questions

1. Who was Bartolomé de Las Casas?

2. What does the Lucayan name, Lukku Cairi, mean?

3. What do the Spanish words, baja mar, (or Bahama) mean?

4. What does the Lucayan name, Bahama, mean?

Ch. 4 ~ How The Bahamas Got its Name

Some years ago, scholars and researchers popularized the idea that the name 'Bahamas' was derived from the Spanish words 'baja mar,' [48] which is today pronounced, 'bahama,' and means 'low tide' or 'shallow sea.' This belief was possibly due to the frequent encounters that early mariners were known to have had with the shallow waters around The Bahamas and the Turks and Caicos Islands.

As stated in the previous chapter, the name 'Bahama' was also the Lucayan name for present day 'Grand Bahama Island' in the northern Bahamas. Some therefore support the idea that the present-day name, 'Bahama' may have been derived from this Lucayan name.[49] However, unlike the Spanish version of the name ('baja mar'), the Lucayan name 'Bahama' is not related to water at all as the name means, 'Large Upper Middle Land.'[50]

However, it is reasonable to believe that The Bahamas got its name from the Spanish words, 'baja mar' with the understanding that the letter 'j' in Spanish is pronounced like the letter 'h' in English. So it would be logical for English speaking persons to spell the words 'baja mar' with an 'h' as in 'Bahama.' On the other hand, the fact that the letter 'h' is used in place of the letter 'j' on Spanish maps as seen in Figure 8 remains a mystery. The answer to the question, 'Why would the Spanish spell a Spanish word (as in 'baja mar') with an English letter (bahamar)?' is perhaps the missing link for solving the mystery of how The Bahamas got its name. Disregarding this unanswered question has rightfully/wrongfully led many to assume that the Spanish words 'baja mar' had somehow evolved overtime to become 'Bahama' and now 'Bahamas.' Consequently, much more research is required in this area.

Nevertheless, the assumption that the name 'Bahamas' is derived from the Spanish words 'baja mar' (meaning 'shallow sea') has some credibility considering that: a). the waters surrounding the Lucayan chain are shallow; b). the first name for the Lucayan archipelago was not 'Bahama'; c). the shallow waters surrounding these islands gave cause for grave concern among early explorers; and d). the name, 'Bahama,' given the island of Grand Bahama by the Lucayans might have reinforced the use of the Spanish words 'baja mar' (at least in part) due to that island's proximity to shallow waters and the similarity of its spelling/pronunciation ('Bahama") to the word 'bajamar.'

The Spanish traditionally gave Spanish names to the lands they claimed on behalf of their monarchs. Although, the Lucayans did have a distinct name for each of the islands in the chain such as Abaco, Exuma, Inagua, Mayaguana, and Samana, they did not, however, have a name (such as the 'Bahama Islands') to represent the entire island chain as a an archipelago. It was not until shortly after Columbus' landfall, early explorers realized that The Bahamas and the Turks and Caicos Islands were a part of the same chain of islands and subsequently gave the archipelago its first name, 'Islas Los Lucayos' [51] (meaning, 'Islands of the Lucayans' or 'Lucayan Islands') after the Lucayans, and not the name 'Bahama.'

Even today, islands within this archipelago are often referred to as the 'Lucayan Islands' by archaeologists, anthropologists, and historians. [52] The Spanish name 'Lucayos' is the shortened form of the name 'Islas de Los Lucayos,' which is Spanish for the name the Lucayan people call themselves, Lukku Cairi[53] or Lucairi,[54] meaning 'Island People.'[55] Today, these 'original Bahamians' are known as 'Lucayans,' which is the English (or Anglicized) version of their Spanish name.

The name 'Lucayos' was perhaps in use before Spanish conquistador Juan Ponce de León embarked upon his famous maritime expedition through the Turks and Caicos Islands and The Bahamas from Puerto Rico in 1513.[56] Some historians claim that Ponce de León went in search of the mythical Fountain of Youth in Bimini, Bahamas. The conquistador's voyage, however, ended with the discovery of Florida making Ponce de León the first European to make landfall in North America at the beginning of a modern era. He named his landfall, Florida, after the Catholic holy day, Pascua de Flores (Feast of Flowers).[57]

The name 'Lucayos' or 'Lucayas' (and not 'Bahama') was often used on early maps to highlight the Lucayan Island chain dating back as early as 1532 around which time

Portuguese cartographer, Diogo Ribero, published his map of the Gulf of Mexico and the 'Islas de Las Lucayas' (Islands of the Lucayans).[58] The same name is also seen on the Spanish map, 'Carta reducida de las islas Lucayas, ò de los Lucayos' that was produced in 1782[59] in Fig. 8.

Also reinforcing the use of the name 'Lucayan Islands' were French cartographers, who also referred to the island chain as 'Isles Lucayes' (or Islands of the Lucayans) as seen on the map, 'Les grandes et petites isles Antilles, et les isles Lucayes avec une partie de la mer du Nord,' which means 'The arge and small Antilles islands, and the Lucayan Islands with a part of the North Sea.' The map was' published in 1779 [60] —over 250 years after the name 'Lucayos' was first used.

The idea that the name 'Bahama' was derived from the Spanish words, 'baja mar', is also strongly supported by the fact that the shallow waters encompassing much of the Lucayan Islands were adjacent to main sea routes that were newly established by European explorers and colonizers.

These sea lanes were frequently used by Spanish treasure ships, as well as other European vessels (such as the French and Dutch) during their return voyages to Europe from the West Indies and the Spanish Mainland in South and Central America. The use of these sea routes would have increased significantly after 1521 when gold and silver were found in abundance among the Aztec and Inca Empires.

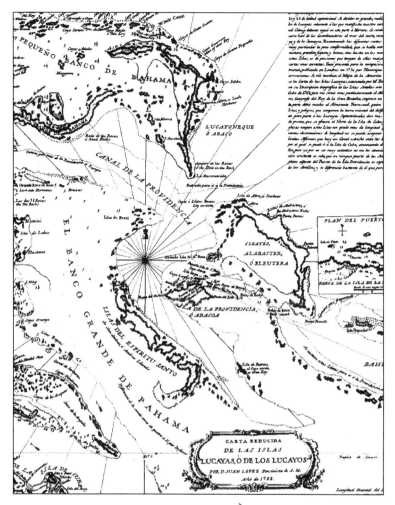

Fig. 8: Map of Islas Lucayas, Ò de Los Lucayos

Maritime routes used included the Old Bahama Channel that runs along the north coast of Cuba near the southern Bahamas, and the 50-mile (80-km) wide 'New Bahama' or 'Bahama Channel' (now known as the Straits of Florida). The

Straits of Florida lie between South Florida's east coast and the Great and Little Bahama Banks. The Bimini Islands are on the western side of the Great Bahama Bank while Grand Bahama Island is on the western side of the Little Bahama Bank. These banks cover vast areas consisting of tens of thousands of square miles of 'shallower' waters from which their names (Great and Little 'Bahama' Bank) may have naturally been derived.

The shallow waters of the Great and Little Bahama Banks would have been etched on the minds of early mariners due to the number of ships that were wrecked, the tons of treasure lost, and the many lives consumed by a watery grave. Interestingly, some of the older maps display the two large banks with their Spanish names; that is, 'El Banco Grande de Bahama' for the 'Great Bank of Bahama,' and 'Pequeño Banco de Bahama' for the 'Little Bank of Bahama' as seen in the 1782 map at Fig. 8.

However, the same map identifies the island chain as 'Islas Lucayas, Ò de Los Lucayos' meaning 'Lucayan Islands.' This strongly suggests that the name 'Bahama' on this map referred only to the shallow waters of The Bahamas, while the name 'Lucayos' referred to the entire island chain, and not the waters that surrounded them.[61] Hence, the name Spanish name, 'Bahama,' meaning 'shallow water' described the 'shallow waters' of the Great and Little Bahama Banks—bearing in mind the Lucayan name, 'Bahama,' (meaning 'Large Upper Middle Land') describes a land mass.

Fig. 9: The Florida Straits with a Part of the Great Bahama Bank

Furthermore, French cartographers identified the Great Bahama Bank with the word 'Pracel'[62]—a Portuguese word that is used when referring to a submerged bank or reef as seen on the map, 'Carte de l'Isle de Cuba et des Isles Lucayes' (meaning Map of Cuba and the Islands of Cuba and the Islands of the Lucayans) published in 1789 by Mentelle. E. (Edme).[63] Later, the name 'Bahama' began to appear along with the name 'Lucayos' or 'Lucayas' and remained so as late as 1855 or possibly later as shown on the 'Map of the West India & Bahama Islands' by British geographer James Wyld that was published in London.[64]

It is worth mentioning that the Lucayan name 'Bahama' as found in today's name, 'Grand Bahama Island' may have also encouraged the use of the Spanish version of the name. Though small in comparison with the American mainland, Grand Bahama Island is the northern most significant landmass on the eastern side of the Straits of Florida. Mariners on their return voyages would have passed Grand Bahama on occasions before heading eastward towards Europe.

It should be noted that this northern Bahamian island borders the southwestern boundary of the Little Bahama Bank where ship wrecks would have occurred. Having renamed a number of the Lucayan islands, it would be of no surprise if the Spanish eventually accepted the Lucayan word 'Bahama' to mean 'baja mar' (or shallow sea) due to its proximity to the shallow waters of the Little Bahama Bank.

Over the years, however, the name 'Bahama' began to replace the name 'Lucayos' or 'Lucayan' on more modern maps. In 1864, for example, A. J. Johnson's highly decorative map of the West Indies and the Caribbean[65] used only the name 'Bahama Islands' to represent The Bahamas and the Turks and Caicos Islands.

Until the question of why the name Bahama is spelled with a 'h' and not a 'j' on a Spanish map, it is reasonable to assume that the shallow waters of The Bahamas (especially

The Lucayan Story

that of the Great and Little Bahama Banks), the deadly encounters that early European mariners had with these shallow waters, and even the Lucayan name (Bahama) given the Lucayan island of Grand Bahama all support the idea that the name, 'Bahamas,' in use today was more than likely derived from the Spanish words, 'baja mar,' meaning 'shallow water' and not the Lucayan name 'Bahama' meaning 'Large Upper Middle Land.'

Questions

1. What is the meaning of the Lucayan word, Bahama?

2. What was the first name given to the chain of islands where The Bahamas and the Turks and Caicos islands are located?

3. What sea routes near The Bahamas did Spanish treasure ships take on their return voyage to Europe?

Ch. 5 ~ Lucayan Ancestry

Historically, the Caribbean was settled by various ethnic groups at different times from mainland South America. These groups had different cultures, which, in some instances, assimilated [17] fully or partially the cultures of others. One such group was the Igneri people who were believed to be the original settlers of the islands of the Lesser Antilles in the southern half of the Caribbean. This Amerindian group was of Arawakan descent from South America and spoke an Arawakan language. According to oral traditions of Caribs in the Lesser Antilles, Igneri settlements were invaded by the Caribs before European arrival. [66]

The defeated Igneri eventually adopted the Carib culture, possibly by the mid-1400s.[67] However, linguistic analysis reveals that the language of the island Caribs was Arawakan. [68] The island Caribs of Martinique and Guadeloupe told the Europeans that they met the Igneri people on these islands where they either killed or drove the men out and made their women their wives. [69] It is also theorized that the Caribs eventually adopted the Arawakan-

---

[17] Assimilate: to adopt the ways of another culture: to fully become part of a different society, country, etc.

Igneri language while maintaining their Carib culture.[70] Today, a number of linguists describe the Carib language as Igneri.[71]

Nevertheless, the Lucayans, Tainos and Caribs were the predominant peoples within the Caribbean region when Christopher Columbus arrived at the dawning of the modern era for the Americas.[72] The Lucayans were a part of the Arawakan language family and were descended from the Tainos of Hispañiola and Cuba. Consequently, some scholars refer to the indigenous people of the Lucayan chain as Lucayan-Taino[73] while others refer to them as Lucayans. The name 'Arawak' was first used by American ethnologist, Daniel Brinton, in 1871 after realizing that the Taino language was part of the Arawakan language group.[74] Christopher Columbus called the Tainos 'Indios' believing that he was in the East Indies.[75]

The Tainos of the northern Caribbean Islands were originally descended from among the Arawak-speaking peoples dwelling on the northeast coast of South America near the Orinoco River in Venezuela[76] (the word 'Arawak' or 'Aruac' means 'meal eater').[77] With the use of dugout canoes, the South American Arawaks slowly made their way up the Caribbean chain to the northern Caribbean Islands in the Greater Antilles where they eventually became known as Tainos.[78] However, the life and culture of the Arawak-speaking tribes in the Caribbean Islands were significantly different from that of the Arawak-speaking tribes of South America.

Fig. 10: Native Carib Indian

Archaeological evidence suggests that The Bahamas and the Turks and Caicos Islands were settled by Tainos sometime between 600 A.D. and 800 A.D.[79] It is also believed that the Tainos from Cuba may have initially settled islands in the central Bahamas,[80] which includes Long Island, while those from Hispañiola may have been primarily responsible for settling the southeastern islands of the Lucayan chain[81] (that is, Inagua and the Turks and Caicos Islands).

From these islands, the native Lucayans eventually went on to settle many of the remaining islands throughout the Lucayan archipelago from Abaco and Grand Bahama in the northern Bahamas to Grand Turk in the Turks and Caicos Islands at the southeastern end of the chain.

After centuries of physical separation from their Taino ancestors in the northern Caribbean, native Tainos, who had settled The Bahamas and the Turks and Caicos Islands, eventually developed a distinct culture where they became known as 'Lucayans.'[82]

Some researchers suggest that other Native Americans had settled the Caribbean [83] from points in North America (Florida),[84] Central America (Yucatan)[85] and South America (Venezuela) prior to the arrival of the Arawak-Tainos, Lucayans and Caribs.[86] Nevertheless, it was the indigenous Lucayans, Tainos and Caribs who dominated the region at the time of Columbus, but later suffered at the hands of Columbus and his European contemporaries.

When Columbus arrived in the Americas, the natives of Hispañiola identified themselves as 'Taino,' which means 'good' or 'noble.'[87] This name was later used by Europeans to distinguish the island-Arawaks from the South American Arawaks.[88] By 1492, the Tainos had settled all of the larger islands of the northern Caribbean or Greater Antilles (that is, Puerto Rico, Hispañiola, Cuba and Jamaica). The Tainos also inhabited several islands in the northern part of the Lesser Antilles in the Caribbean chain, which included the Virgin Islands, St. Kitts and Nevis, and Antigua and Barbuda.

Today, the Tainos of Puerto Rico, Hispañiola and Eastern Cuba are referred to as Classic Taino. Those of Central Cuba and Jamaica are classified as Western Taino, while those of the northernmost part of the Lesser Antilles just east of Puerto Rico are called Eastern Taino.[89] Language and culture varied among these Taino groups.[90]

The Taino of Hispañiola called their enemies from the east, 'Caribs;'[91] the name Carib means strong or brave person[92]. However, these island-Caribs originally called themselves 'Kallinago' in their native men's language or 'Kalliponam' in their native women's language.[93] The Spanish word for 'Carib' was 'Caribe' and the French equivalent was 'Galibi.'[94] The name Carib was later imposed on these native islanders by European 'outsiders.'[95]

Columbus was the first European to make mention of the Caribs in his diary during his first voyage to the Americas.[96] The collective name for the islands of the region (the Caribbean Islands) and the sea they embrace (the Caribbean Sea) were derived from the name 'Carib,' which was a name given to these war-faring people by the Tainos and popularized by European explorers. By the time Columbus arrived in the region, the Caribs had already settled a number of Caribbean Islands between Guadeloupe and Saint Vincent in the Windward Islands of the Caribbean, and were steadily migrating northward along the eastern Caribbean chain toward the Greater Antilles.

The Caribs were a war-faring people known to capture Tainos from the Greater Antilles (Puerto Rico or Hispañiola) as prisoners of war, which added to the influx of Arawakan speakers to Carib communities.[97] Some scholars suggest that the people who inflicted war wounds upon the Lucayans whom Columbus first met in the Bahamas may have been Caribs or possibly Tainos from Hispañiola.[98]

Based on the initial description given him by the Taino people of their Carib raiders, Columbus assumed the Caribs were cannibals.[99] In fact, the name 'Carib' came from the Taino words 'cariba' and 'caniba.'[100] European interpreters confused the word 'Caniba' with the Latin root word, 'canis' (meaning of or related to a dog), and naturally assumed that this word made reference to a dog-headed monster, which reinforced the idea that the Caribs were cannibals.[101] The word 'cannibal' first appears in Columbus' journal on 23rd November 1492, which was documented during his second voyage to the New World.[102] The name Carib eventually became 'Canibs' and synonymous with the word 'cannibal' or 'man-eater.'[103]

Nevertheless, Europeans had no firsthand account of Caribs being cannibalistic predators or 'New World savages'[104] other than that which might have been associated with the ritual eating of relatives after they died.[105] The notion of Caribs being man-eaters gave Columbus and his contemporaries some justification to enslave them. [106] Consequently, hundreds of Caribs were captured and transported as slaves to Hispañiola.[107] It is interesting to note that in 2015, the Carib Reserve in Dominic [108]—a Caribbean Island in the Lesser Antilles with approximately 3,000 Carib descendants—has since reverted[18] to using the name 'Kalinago' "to reflect a better indigenous identity, to dispel the historic negative connotations linked with the word Carib..."

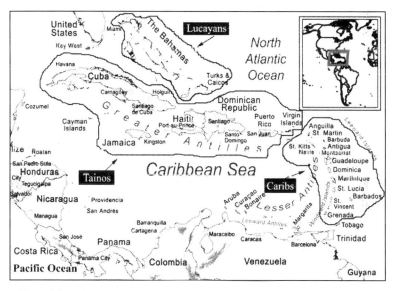

Fig. 11: Islands occupied by Lucayans, Tainos & Caribs

---

[18] Revert: to come or go back (as to a former condition, period, or subject).

Like the Arawaks, the island-Caribs also originated from the northern shores of South America where their ancestors were known as 'Kariña' or 'Kalina.'[109] Although they spoke Cariban, their language belonged to the same broad Arawakan language of the Tainos of Hispañiola and the Arawaks of South America.[110] The Cariban language family may have comprised up to three dozen languages mainly around the northern Amazon area.[111] Caribs still exist today in several countries near the north coast of South America. Among these countries are Venezuela, Guyana, Surinam and French Guiana.[112]

Some of the Caribbean Islands inhabited by Tainos at the time of Columbus were mainly islands of the Greater Antilles and included Cuba, Jamaica, Hispaniola (Haiti and Dominican Republic), Puerto Rico, and the Virgin Islands. Islands inhabited by the Caribs at the time of Columbus were mostly those among the Lesser Antilles. These included the Virgin Islands [113], St. Kitts & Neves[114] (where the Kalinagos offered resistance to the British and French on St. Kitts), Dominica, Martinique, Antigua and Barbuda, and St. Vincent & the Grenadines.

Questions

1. Which continent did the Arawaks and Caribs come from?

2. Who were the main indigenous groups of people living in the Caribbean when early European explorers arrived in the region?

3. Which indigenous people were believed to have been cannibals?

Ch. 6 ~ The Lucayan People

"They seem to live in that golden world of which the old writers speak so much, wherein men lived simply and innocently without enforcement of laws, without quarrelling, judges and libels, content only to satisfy nature." Peter Martyr[115]

Fig. 12: Lucayan Indians (Courtesy of T. Bethel)

Prior to the arrival of Columbus in The Bahamas, many of the islands of the Lucayan archipelago were settled by the friendly Lucayan people with an estimated population of 20,000 to 40,000 people. These Amerindian descendants of the Arawak-Tainos had populated the Lucayan Islands for at least 600 years before European contact. Unlike the mountainous, big island life of their Taino descendants, the Lucayans lived in much smaller communities [116] on flat islands with the highest elevation being Mount Alvernia, also known as Como Hill, on Cat Island some 206 feet (or 62.8 meters) high.

The Lucayans were a friendly people and 'lovers of peace'[117] whose lifestyles were similar in many ways to that of their Taino counterparts. However, their way of life among the less fertile, smaller islands of The Bahamas had evolved into a distinct culture over the centuries.[118] Each inhabited Lucayan Island consisted of small communities or villages that were headed by Caciques. [119] The Caciques were chieftains responsible for the political and religious affairs of their respective villages. [120] Their four-legged, low-lying ceremonial stools (or duhos) that were made of stone or wood represented their seat of authority.[121]

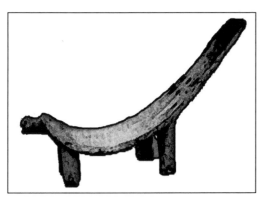

Fig. 13: Duho—A Ceremonial Chair (Courtesy T. Bethel)

In comparison, the islands of the northern Caribbean were divided into much larger territories, each ruled by a Cacique. The Taino Caciques had no political or religious control over the Lucayan Islands. The Arawaks believed in an eternal paradise called coyaba—a place of pleasure where the Caribs would be their servants. The Spanish lured unsuspecting Lucayans aboard their ships as captives under the pretense that they would be repatriated to coyaba.[122] They also believed in spirits called Zemis that lived in trees, carved images and relics of the dead. Devils were often in the shape of a monkey or an owl. Fortune or misfortune meant that the spirits were pleased or displeased.[123]

Fig.14 : Lucayan Dugout Canoe at The Bahamas Historical Society and Museum (Courtesy T. Bethel)

In contrast with their Taino counterparts, the Lucayans were less familiar with warfare. Being further north of the Caribbean, their islands were less subject to the attacks by their war-faring counterparts, the Caribs. They knew nothing of iron or swords.[124] Columbus did note that several of the Lucayans on San Salvador had scars about their bodies which they claimed were from "people from neighbouring islands who wanted to capture them...."[125]

Some suggest that these attacks could have come from one of at least three groups of people. One possible group was the Caribs, who were the arch enemies of the Taino people.[126] These war-faring people had already worked their way northward from South America through the smaller islands of the Lesser Antilles in the southern half of the Caribbean. By the 1450s, they were launching successful raids on Puerto Rico and Hispañiola in the Greater Antilles of the northern Caribbean chain[127]. Another possible group could have been Tainos from the Greater Antilles, and the third possibility could have been Indians from Florida.[128]

Thinking he had arrived in the Far East, Columbus believed the Lucayans were Indians.[129] These native Amerindians were described as being brown-skinned, handsome and physically fit in appearance. Their foreheads were flattened shortly after birth, which they believed provided added protection against the blows of enemies.[130] Their long, straight, black hair was 'as course as a horse's tail' and covered their flattened foreheads as far as the eyebrows.[131] Lucayans wore little clothing and went about almost naked. The men wore loin cloths and the women short mantle skirts.[132]

Foods the Lucayans ate were either indigenous to The Bahamas or initially imported from the northern Caribbean. Fruits included pineapple, guava, tamarind, guinep and papaya. Corn, peas, yam, and potatoes were among the vegetables eaten. Cassava (or manioc) was a dietary staple.[133]

Tobacco—a name derived from the Tainos—may have also been among the crops grown by Lucayans.[134] The Spaniards were first introduced to smoking tobacco by the Tainos of Cuba. The Lucayans called the plant cohiba. The leaves

The Lucayan Story

were rolled and smoked like cigars. However, the Y-shaped pipe that was inserted into their nostrils while smoking was called 'tabaco.' The Spaniards adopted the habit, which spread world-wide in the years that followed.[135] The Lucayans were also agile hunters and very skilled at diving. In 1508, large numbers of Lucayans were taken as slaves by the Spanish to Cubagua, a small island off the Venezuelan Caribbean coast to dive for pearls.[136] Meats eaten by the Lucayans included conch (a sea mollusk now popular in Bahamian diet), agouti (related to the rabbit; called utia by the Lucayans), fish, and turtle.[137] Pottery used was made from burnt shells and is described as Palmetto Ware.[138] They were known to engage in trade among the Lucayan Islands, as well as the northern Caribbean islands of Hispañiola (Haiti) and Cuba using dug-out canoes that transported up to 150 rowers.[139]

Lucayan homes were made of wood and were either round with cone-shaped roofs or rectangular in shape. The roofs were also thatched with palm branches.[140] Some of these homes accommodated extended families consisting of up to 20 persons in some cases.[141] For recreation, Lucayans enjoyed singing and dancing, which they called 'arieto' and drank beer made from cassava or maize.[142]

They also played a ball game known as 'batos.' During the sport, opposing teams were required to keep a rubber-like ball in the air using their feet, knees and hips only. No hands were allowed to touch the ball.[143] Remnants of former Lucayan sites and artifacts were found throughout The Bahamas.[144] Although, the Lucayans were a friendly people, their carefree lifestyle would soon be lost with the advent of European explorers,

The Lucayan Story

Fig. 15: Replica of a Lucayan House, Leon Levy Native Plant Preserve, Eleuthera, Bahamas. (Courtesy T. Bethel)

Questions

1. What was the approximate number of Arawaks living in The Bahamas and the Turks and Caicos Islands at the time of Columbus?

2. List three foods that the Lucayans ate?

3. What did the Lucayans call their leaders?

Ch. 7 ~ Populating the Americas

Interestingly enough, the word 'tourist' comes from the word 'tour,'[145] which means 'to travel about.'[146] The word 'travel' comes from the word 'travail,'[147] which originally meant suffering.[148] In the original sense of the word, a tourist is someone on a quest for a better life that many call paradise.

Several theories suggest how the Americas were populated by the ancient spread of civilization. The most credible of these theories indicate that human civilization first reached the Americas from East Asia, which corresponds with archaeological finds and DNA data collected by National Geographic's Genographic Project. The Genographic Project is a research initiative that traces the ancestry of human genes to determine migration paths of ancestors of modern-day humans.[149]

The widely accepted land bridge (Beringia) theory suggests that the ancient trek of human civilization began on the continent of Africa and then made its way through the continents of Asia and Europe before crossing the Bering land bridge that once joined the northeastern end of Russia with the western end of Alaska.[150] Ancient civilization then trekked southward through North, Central and South America.[151] (One researcher suggests it took 1,000 years for human civilization to travel from Alaska in the north to the southern tip of South America.)[152] Upon reaching South

America, an offshoot of spreading civilization (an Arawak-speaking people) island-hopped its way northward along the Caribbean chain.

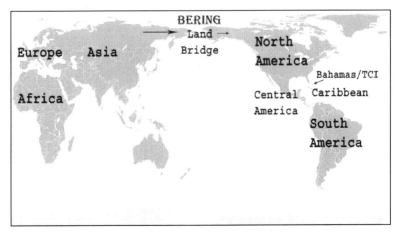

Fig. 16: Bering Land Bridge (Beringia)

These Arawaks traveled northward from the northern coast of South America and eventually settled a number of northern Caribbean Islands, which included Puerto Rico, Hispañiola, Jamaica and Cuba (in the Greater Antilles) where they became known as Taino. Some of the Taino people later migrated from Hispañiola and Cuba to The Bahamas and the Turks and Caicos Islands from as early as 600 A.D., where they later became known as Lucayans.

It is speculated that the Ciboney (also spelled Siboney) people might have settled some of the islands in the Bahama chain before the Lucayans arrived. However, there is too little archaeological evidence and firsthand records to verify this idea.[153] However, historical evidence suggests that the Ciboney people inhabited Cuba prior to the arrival of the Tainos, and later coexisted alongside the Taino people in western Cuba.[154] Nevertheless, the Lucayans were the only people known to have inhabited The Bahamas and the Turks and Caicos Islands during European contact.

Some researchers argue that the Americas may have also been populated by indigenous peoples from several points in Asia and the Pacific (including Australia). [155] Others hypothesize that the Americas may have been populated by people from southeast Europe by way of the Atlantic Ocean. [156] However, most population theories generally agree that human civilization reached the continents of the Americas last by migrating east from the Asian continent.

Genetic research also supports the idea that the Americas were populated by an eastward migration from Asia that originated in Africa. This spread of human civilization has characterized humanity's continued quest for a better life.

With the permanent settling of North America, Central America, South America and the Caribbean Islands, the eventual arrival of the Lucayans in the Lucayan Chain of Islands represented the end of this eastward trek of human civilization in its quest for a better life that many call 'Paradise' near the beginning of the modern era in human history.

Coincidentally, the island that is just off the north coast of New Providence, was renamed Paradise Island in 1962. Paradise Island was previously named, Hog Island.[157] Today, this island is home to the world-famous Atlantis Paradise Resort, which boasts 'the world's largest open-air marine habitat' and is visited annually by thousands from around the world in their quest for Paradise.[158]

Questions

    1. Where is Beringia?

2. Where did the first people who settled the Americas come from?

3. Explain briefly how the Americas became populated with indigenous peoples?

Ch. 8 ~ Old World Meets New World

Before Spanish explorers arrived in the New World, the indigenous Lucayan people basked in a fairly tranquil existence, living in harmony with their natural environment and in relative peace with each other on these verdant lands.

Fig. 17: Columbus' Initial Voyage to the New World
(Courtesy of T. Bethel)

Physically separated from their homelands in Hispañiola and Cuba for hundreds of years, the Lucayans evolved into a distinct community of resourceful craftspeople who organized their trade routes, grew cassava and cotton, and formed their own government. Like the Tainos, the Lucayans spoke a variant of the Arawakan language. Sadly, their ideas of a peaceful existence came to an abrupt end not long after welcoming Christopher Columbus to their shores.

Fig. 18: Columbus' Statue Government House, Nassau Bahamas (Courtesy of T. Bethel)

The Lucayan Story

Columbus was an Italian explorer who, unlike his contemporaries, devised a plan to reach the gold and spices of the Far East by sailing west across the Atlantic Ocean from Spain. For Columbus, the Atlantic crossing was a worthwhile venture compared to the excessive time, costs and hazards of crossing the overland Silk Road that was under Arab control.[159]

Furthermore, the sea route to the East Indies from the south coast of Africa was unknown to European explorers at the time. Columbus' plan was eventually accepted and funded by King Ferdinand and Queen Isabella of Spain in 1492, after several years in search of financing from the European Crowns of England, Portugal and Spain.

The year 1492 was a time of quests and conquests for Spain. It was the year that the Spanish monarchs drove out the last invading armies of the North African Muslim Moors from the Iberian Peninsula to regain control of Spain after 700 years of Muslim occupation.[160] 1492 also marked the closing chapter of the Middle Ages (or the Medieval period)— the period that immediately preceded the Modern Age, which commenced around 1500.[161] The year 1492 was also the year when Columbus set sail for the East Indies.

As part of the royal agreement, Columbus was granted the title Admiral of the Ocean Sea along with a share of any wealth he discovered. Columbus' mission also included the Christianizing of the peoples of the Indies.[162] Almost seventy days after departing the port of Palos in southwest Spain, Columbus' expeditionary vessels (the Niña, Pinta and the flagship, Santa Maria) made their first landfall in the Americas on a tiny island in the Lucayan chain on 12 October, 1492.

Upon making landfall, Columbus was greeted by the peaceful Lucayans. The Italian navigator then claimed the island for the Catholic monarchs of Spain, who sponsored his expedition. Columbus also renamed the island of his historic landfall San Salvador—Spanish for Holy Savior (in reference to Jesus Christ, who according to Biblical text is the Prince of Peace). The island's original Lucayan name was 'Guanahani'[163] meaning 'Place of the Iguana.' [164]

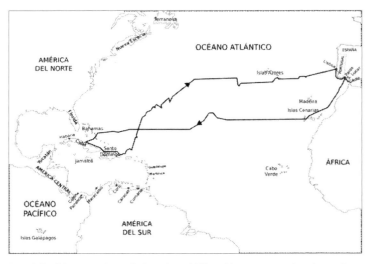

Fig. 19: Christopher Columbus' First Voyage to the Americas

While at San Salvador, Columbus noted that the Lucayans would make "good servants"[165] and that these indigenous people were "very unskilled in arms."[166] Columbus' initial actions in claiming the land for the Spanish Crown and his assessment of the Lucayan vulnerabilities represented the first seeds of slavery to be planted in the minds of European explorers, thereby foreshadowing the demise of the Lucayan people.

The Lucayan Story

Names Given to Bahamian Islands by Christopher Columbus

Lucayan Name[167]	Columbus Name	Current Name
Guanahani	San Salvador	San Salvador
Yuma	Fernandina	Long Island
Maniwa	Santa María de la Concepción	Rum Cay
Yabake	Isabella	Crooked Island

Questions

1. Who financed Columbus' voyage?

2. What was Columbus' intended destination after setting sail from Spain in 1492?

3. What is the Lucayan name for the island of Columbus' first landfall in the New World and what does that name mean?

Ch. 9 ~ Other New World Explorers

Prior to Columbus' arrival in the Americas, Leif Erikson, a Norseman from Iceland, sailed west to North America after leaving Greenland during a maritime expedition.[168] Erikson made landfall on Newfoundland, Canada in 1000 A.D., some 500 years before Columbus arrived in the Americas and approximately 200 to 400 years after the Lucayans had settled the Lucayan archipelago. However, Erikson's contact with Native Americans was short-lived and did not affect any lasting change on the destiny of the Americas or the world.

Earlier still, in his book entitled, 1421: The Year China Discovered the World, former British Royal Navy Officer, Gavin Menzies, argues that the Chinese Admiral Zhen He arrived in the Americas by sailing west across the Atlantic ocean from the African continent. Menzies also claims that Admiral He's fleet arrived in the Americas approximately seventy years before Columbus.[169] According to Menzies, Admiral He's fleet had also sailed through The Bahamas.[170] However, scholars, including Chinese authorities, argue that Menzies' theory lacks credible evidence.[171]

Historians also argue that Africans were another group of pre-Columbian explorers from outside the Americas. Historical data and archaeological evidence suggest that Africans from the west coast of Africa sailed to the Americas from as early as 200 B.C., around the time of the Mayans.

Fig. 20: Norseman Leif Erikson

It is further suggested that the ocean currents and winds between Africa and the Americas made this voyage possible, as they did centuries later for Columbus and his vessels. Based on historical accounts, these Africans had settled in Central and South America where they were believed to have existed up until the time of early European arrival in the Americas.[172] Here again, any presence of early Africans in the Americas did not change world events in any substantial way.

Unlike the short-lived encounter Native Americans had with European Norsemen or with any other foreign explorer, most researchers agree that it was the historic meeting between Columbus and the Lucayans in the Lucayan chain that ultimately led to the transformation of the Americas, which forever changed the course of modern history and human destiny.[173]

Fig. 21: Chinese Admiral Zhen He

The organizers of the 1992 Smithsonian's Seeds of Change exhibit described the encounter between the two civilizations (that is, European and Native American) as 'not a story of the discovery of the New World by the Old World' but rather a 'story of an encounter between two branches of humankind that diverged from each other ....'[174]

The Bahamas and the Turks and Caicos Islands therefore mark the spot where the reunion of the two branches of civilization—Native Americans and Europeans—took place. This historic meeting resulted in the permanent reconnection between civilizations that had initially spread out in opposite directions after thousands of years. It was this reunion that ushered in a new era for the Americas from the shores of the Lucayan Islands at the beginning of modern history. The advent of this new beginning was underscored by the naming of the entire Western Hemisphere (the Americas) after the European explorer Amerigo Vespucci, who first recognized that Columbus had 'discovered' a New World.[175]

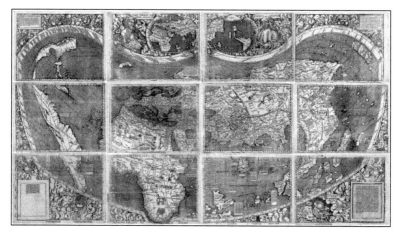

Fig. 22: Waldseemüller Map of 1507 showing America as being separate from Asia

Questions

1. Who was Leif Erikson?

2. What other people or race is believed to have reached the Americas before Columbus did?

3. What major event permanently reunited world civilizations in the Americas?

Ch. 10 ~ San Salvador Island

For over 200 years, historians have debated which island in the Lucayan archipelago is the actual site of Columbus' first landfall in the Americas.[176] At least eight or more possible sites in The Bahamas and the Turks and Caicos Islands have since been proposed.[177] In The Bahamas, these sites include Watling's Island,[178] which now carries the name San Salvador Island, along with Samana Cay and Cat Island, which are all located in the central Bahamas.[179]

Robert Fuson, Professor Emeritus of Geography at the University of South Florida in Tampa, is a former advocate of the Grand Turk landfall site. Professor Fuson argues that there have been 30 proposed sites over 300 years with only three of these proposals having been changed during this time frame.[180] However, the majority of these proposals support Columbus making landfall in the Bahama Islands.

San Salvador Island (formerly, Watling's Island) is located in the central Bahamas approximately 350 miles (563 km) southeast of Miami, Florida. The island is about 13 miles (20 km) long and five miles (8 km) wide with a population of about 940 people (2010 Census). In 1803, the name 'San Salvador' was transferred from Watling's Island to Cat Island as St. Salvador.[181] The small island located just off the northwest coast of Cat Island still carries the name Little

The Lucayan Story

San Salvador (also known as Half Moon Cay)—a reminder of Cat Island's ties with its past.[182]

However, in May 1926, The Bahamas' legislature renamed Watling's Island, San Salvador, thus making that island The Bahamas' official site of Columbus' first landfall.[183] This latter naming campaign was backed by Father Chrysostom Schreiner, an American Catholic priest who was shipwrecked on Watling's Island in January 1892.[184]

Other sites reputed to be Columbus' first landfall are found in the Turks and Caicos Islands.[185] These sites include Grand Turk and East Caicos.[186] In 1825, Martín Fernández de Navarrete was the first to suggest that the first landfall was Grand Turk. However, some like Professor Fuson argue that there is no scientific evidence to support this claim for the Turks and Caicos Islands.[187]

In his article, The Turks and Caicos Islands as Possible Landfall Sites for Columbus, Professor Fuson claims that there are no more supporters for the Caicos site and only two remain for the Grand Turk site. He concludes that based on the findings of intensive investigations initiated by the Society for the History of Discoveries and completed by the National Geographic Society, Grand Turk has been ruled out and that Samana Cay northeast of Crooked Island in The Bahamas is the most likely landfall site.[188]

To date, the archaeological excavation undertaken by Dr. Charles Hoffman during 1983 to 1985 has revealed that the only site in the Bahama chain where 15th century Spanish paraphernalia exists alongside Lucayan items is on present-day San Salvador Island in The Bahamas.[189]

The Lucayan Story

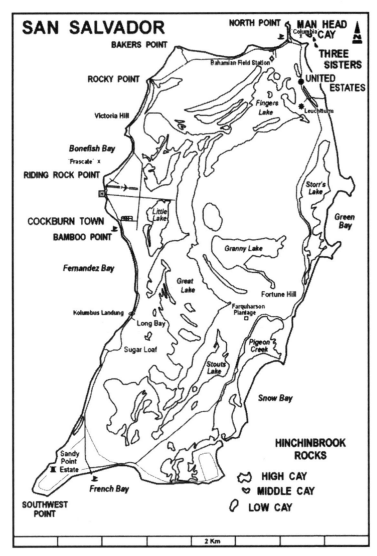

Fig. 23: San Salvador Island

Although debate continues over the location of Columbus' first landfall in the Americas, it is generally agreed that the historic event took place in the Lucayan chain of islands[190] of which The Bahamas and the Turks and Caicos Islands are a part.

Fig. 24: Monument presented by Spain, Landfall Park, San Salvador Island

Questions

1. What year was Watlings Island officially named San Salvador?

2. List three Islands that were believed to be islands where Columbus made his first landfall?

3. Which island to date is the only place where both Spanish and Lucayan artifacts were found in the Lucayan chain?

Ch. 11 ~ A Quest for Gold

Columbus was in search of an alternative route to access the wealth of the East Indies. The little gold ornaments worn by the friendly Lucayans who welcomed Columbus to their shores got his immediate attention after he made an unintended landfall on San Salvador Island in the Lucayan chain.[191] Believing that he was in the East Indies, Columbus made inquiries about where gold could be found.

The Lucayans pointed south-southwest toward Cuba,[192] which Columbus presumed to be Cipangu (Japan)—a place of "extensive trade, gold, spices, great shipping, and merchants."[193] After spending fifteen days sailing through the islands in the central and southern Bahama chain, Columbus headed in a southwesterly direction, eventually arriving off the north coast of Cuba, which he mistakenly identified as Cathay (China)[194].

Columbus continued his voyage eastward until he made landfall on an island that the native Tainos called Ayiti (now spelled, Haiti) on 5 December, 1492. The European explorer then renamed the island La Isla Española (now Hispaniola, the island of the Republic of Haiti and the Dominican Republic).[195] By the time Columbus arrived in the Americas, the indigenous Tainos of Hispaniola had divided the island into five dominions, with each dominion headed by a Taino chief or 'cacique.'[196] Today, one-third of Hispaniola is occupied by the Republic of Haiti on its western side and the remaining two-thirds is occupied by the Dominican Republic on the eastern side.

Not long after being greeted by the Tainos of Hispañiola, Columbus discovered gold. On Christmas Eve (24 December 1492), Columbus' flagship, the Santa Maria, ran aground while in waters off Hispañiola's north coast. Columbus was forced to leave about thirty-nine of his men behind to build a garrison named La Navidad near what is now Cap-Haïtien on the north coast of Haiti. La Navidad became the first European attempt to establish a permanent settlement in the Americas at the onset of a new era.[197] Columbus and the remainder of his crew returned to Palos, Spain on 5 March 1493 aboard the Niña and the Pinta with news of their findings, thus ending the explorer's first voyage to the Americas.

Upon returning to the Americas during his second voyage later in November 1493, Columbus discovered that the native Tainos had killed the men he had left behind to look for gold.[198] A new Spanish colony named Isabella was then established east of La Navidad on the north coast. The colony at Santo Domingo was later founded on the south side of the island. As a result of a sustained Spanish presence, Hispañiola became the nurturing ground of the modern Americas during its early period of development.[199]

Although Columbus took possession of The Bahamas and the Turks and Caicos Islands on behalf of Spain during his first landfall in the Americas in 1492, the Spanish Crown never settled the peaceful islands. Columbus, nevertheless, continued his quest to discover the vast riches of what he mistakenly believed to be the East Indies. It was the English who were the first to reclaim these islands from as early as 1629 after the Spanish neglected them.[200] However, no real effort to settle them was made by the English until 1648

The Lucayan Story

with the arrival of the Eleutherian Adventurers from Bermuda.[201]

Altogether, Columbus made a total of four voyages to the Americas with his final voyage ending on 7 November 1504.[202] During his 12 years of exploring the New World, the Italian navigator ventured as far south as Trinidad and the northern coast of Venezuela, and as far west as Honduras in Central America, but Columbus never saw or made landfall on the North American continent. Nevertheless, the capital of the United States of America, the District of Columbia, was named in his honor by 1791.[203]

In 1506—two years following his last voyage to the New World—Columbus died believing that he had discovered a new route to the East Indies by sailing west from Spain. The Italian navigator was 55 years old at the time of his death. Columbus never returned to the tiny islands of the Lucayan archipelago after making his first landfall in the Americas on one of their shores in 1492.

It was not until the Italian explorer Amerigo Vespucci arrived in the Americas in 1499 that it became apparent that Columbus had in fact discovered a world that was entirely new to Europeans. This 'New World' was later named after Amerigo Vespucci.[204] It was the German cartographer, Martin Waldseemüller, who began printing the name 'America' on New World maps he produced in 1507[205]—the year following Columbus' death.

Questions

1. What part of the world did Columbus believe he was in when he made landfall in the Americas in 1492?

2. What happened to the men who were left behind on the island of Hispañiola by Columbus during Columbus' first voyage to the Americas?

3. Why didn't the Spanish colonize The Bahamas and the Turks and Caicos Islands?

Ch. 12 ~ Lucayan Demise

"They err who count it glorious to subdue By conquest far and wide, to overrun Large countries, and in field great battles win, Great cities by assault. What do these worthies But rob and spoil, burn, slaughter, and enslave Peaceable nations, neighbouring or remote, Made captive, yet deserving freedom more Than those their conquerors, who leave behind Nothing but ruin wheresoe'er they rove, And all the flourishing works of peace destroy." Paradise Regained, John Milton.[206]

European enslavement of Native Americans (Tainos) actually began in Hispañiola during Columbus' second voyage to the Americas in 1493. [207] Thus began the centuries-long robbing, spoiling, burning, slaughtering and enslaving of the Amerindians by foreign invaders in the modern Americas. Increased demands for slave labor by the early 1500s resulted in organized slave raids by the Spanish.

Effective resistance to early European incursions by the Caribs of the smaller Caribbean Islands of the Lesser Antilles and the Arawakan tribes of South America made it more challenging for the Spanish. [208] The mountainous areas where many Caribs lived also made it difficult for the European invaders to capture them.[209]

Even the Tainos of Hispañiola fought against Spanish militias with well-organized and equipped warriors. On one occasion, some 15,000 Taino warriors confronted Columbus' forces during his second voyage to the Americas.[210] Strong resistance was also offered by the Taino Cacique (chief), Hatuey. Originally from Hispañiola, Hatuey later fled to Cuba where Spanish forces captured and killed him in 1512.[211]

Hatuey had witnessed the indiscriminate slaughter of hundreds of innocent Tainos; he also realized that gold was the god that the Spanish worshipped and were all too willing to kill others for it. Just prior to his execution, the Spaniards gave Hatuey the option of going to heaven by converting to Christianity. [212] Upon being told that he would meet Spaniards in heaven should he decide to go there, Hatuey opted to go to hell. [213] Ironically, the brutality the Amerindians suffered under European oppression was never advocated by the Head of the Christian Faith (Jesus Christ) whom the Europeans claimed to worship. [214]

The Taino rebel, Enriquillo, was more successful in preventing the Spanish invaders from defeating his warriors after a 13-year standoff with the Spanish, which ended in a truce in 1533. Nevertheless, Spanish forces destroyed the Taino civilization and their way of life in the Greater and Lesser Antilles.[215]

Not long after Columbus' departure from the Lucayan chain in 1492, Spanish forces took little time in depopulating the islands of the indigenous Lucayans. Unlike the Caribs and the Tainos, the Lucayans were a simple and relatively peaceful people[216] whose small, flat islands made them easy prey for slave raids.

Fig. 25: Forms of European Torture

Enslavement of the indigenous populations initially began in Hispañiola with the Tainos before spreading to Cuba and Puerto Rico. The subsequent dwindling of these native populations in the northern Caribbean Islands resulted in a demand for slave labor outside the Greater Antilles. Hence, Spanish explorers began to look to the 'Lucayos' (or the Lucayan islands) as a potential source of slave labor.[217] Here, the more passive and defenseless Lucayans were easier to capture. The Lucayans were subsequently enslaved and forced to work in 'gold mining enterprises' in the Greater Antilles. They were also skilled at diving and many were forced to engage in the pearl-diving industry off Cubagua near the Caribbean coast of north Venezuela.[218]

Within seven years of Columbus' departure from the Lucayan islands, the seeds of slavery that were first planted in the minds of the Spanish on the shores of San Salvador during Columbus' first landfall in the Americas had finally grown and begun to bear fruit. In 1499, the Italian explorer Amerigo Vespucci (a contemporary of Columbus) raided these islands and captured 232 Lucayans.[219] In 1509—three years following Columbus' death—the enslaving of Lucayans was fully sanctioned by the Spanish monarch, King Ferdinand.[220] "Within a generation" of Columbus' landfall, virtually all of the 20,000 (or possibly up to 40,000[221]) Lucayans were eradicated from these peaceful shores.[222]

Many of the Lucayans that were carried away as slaves died alongside their Taino relatives as a result of cruel and inhumane treatment, foreign diseases, executions and starvation. Some researchers believe that The Bahamas and the Turks and Caicos Islands were depopulated by 1530.[223] It is speculated that some Lucayan sites might have existed in the Lucayan chain up until the mid-1500s.[224] By 1513, however, the Spanish Conquistador Juan Ponce de León saw only one elderly Lucayan as he sailed through the Lucayan islands. That same year, Ponce de León went on to become the first modern-era European to make landfall on the east Florida coast in the southern United States of America.[225]

In 1520, the Spanish were unsuccessful in finding any Lucayans in the Lucayan islands during their slave raids.[226] It is suggested that the Lucayans were long-extinct in the

Bahama archipelago and other Caribbean Islands by 1550.[227] To date, there are no historical records that indicate the Lucayans still existed in The Bahamas and the Turks and Caicos Islands at the time Bermudians settled the islands in 1648.

The Spanish slave raiding expeditions resulted in the Lucayans becoming the first among the indigenous peoples of the modern Americas to be uprooted from their homeland by European explorers and to suffer total genocide. The Bahamas and the Turks and Caicos Islands were therefore depopulated and left abandoned for more than a century until they were resettled by British colonists from Bermuda in 1648. The first Bermudian settlers to The Bahamas were led by William Sayle, who was a British sea captain as well as a former governor of Bermuda and a Puritan. Governor Sayle led seventy settlers from Bermuda to The Bahamas in search of religious freedom.[228]

Spanish colonists, however, soon turned their attention towards African slave labor as the indigenous Taino, Lucayan and Carib populations died out or escaped capture in the Caribbean Islands. By 1510, African slaves were being systematically shipped to the Greater Antilles with the approval of the Spanish crown.[229]

The first Africans to arrive in The Bahamas came with the first European settlers in 1648 by way of Bermuda. They were very few in number. These numbers, however, began to increase with the arrival of additional British settlers from Barbados and Bermuda in the early 1700s. Many of the early black settlers in The Bahamas were believed to be free men.[230]

The number of African slaves and free blacks increased by the thousands when thousands of American loyalists (supporters of the British Crown) came to The Bahamas to escape 'the inequities of peace' brought about by the

American War of Independence. These loyalists also brought their slaves with them.[231] Like the indigenous peoples who preceded them, the imported Africans and their descendants suffered similar atrocities of slavery, which continued well into the 1800s before being abolished by European powers.[232]

Questions

1. Why was it difficult for the early European explorers to defeat the Tainos and the Caribs of the Caribbean?

2. Why were the Lucayans easily taken as slaves?

3. What year in recorded history did the Spanish first return to the Lucayan Islands to capture Lucayans?

4. Why was it necessary to import Africans as slaves?

Ch. 13 ~ The Black Seminoles

Some are inclined to believe that not all of the Lucayan Indians died out during the era of 'discovery' in the Americas. As mentioned in the previous chapter, there is currently no available evidence to support this belief. However there are a group of Native Americans that made The Bahamas their home during the 1800s. This group consisted of Seminole Indians and Black Seminole Indians.

Ironically, not all runaway African slaves in the United States sought refuge in the northern States or Canada. Some fled to Florida where they made their home among the Seminole Indians—a mixed group of Native American Tribes—north of St. Augustine, Florida. Florida was the sovereign territory of Spain from the 1600s.[233] The presence of black slaves in Florida led to the creation of a racially mixed people with a new identity for their offspring known as the Black Seminoles.[234]

In 1819, Florida became the territory of the United States and the Seminoles were driven to Indian Reserves. Runaway slaves dreaded the thought of being retaken as slaves by their white masters.[235] However, during the early 1800s, Seminoles and Black Seminoles sought refuge among the Bahama Islands. After several futile attempts of getting help from the British authorities in The Bahamas, the Seminole alliance clandestinely[19] made their way to the west coast of North Andros aboard canoes in 1821 where they remained undiscovered by Bahamian authorities for seven years. (The Bahamas was a British Colony at the time the black Indians arrived.)

Fig. 26: Black Seminoles

Over time, these descendants of Native Americans and Africans established a local community which today is

---

[19] Clandestinely: done in a private place or way: done secretly.

known as Red Bays.[236] The Seminoles and Black Seminoles have since become socially and culturally integrated with native populations throughout Andros and The Bahamas. Unlike the Lucayans, however, neither the Black slaves nor the Seminoles ever suffered total genocide.

Questions:
1. Why did some of the black slaves of America escape to Florida?

2. Who were the Seminole Indians?

3. Why did the Seminole Indians come to The Bahamas and where did they settle?

Ch. 14 ~ Gold Rush of the Americas

The accidental meeting of the westward and eastward treks of human civilizations on the shores of the Lucayan archipelago was celebrated as a glorious opportunity for economic growth and expansion for Spain and the other European powers that followed. For the Lucayans and most of the indigenous peoples of the Americas, however, this momentous occasion marked the beginning of the end for their way of life.

The initial discovery of gold in Hispañiola by Columbus became the catalyst for Spain's colonization of the Americas. Colonization got under way during Columbus' second voyage to the New World in 1493. During his second voyage, Columbus returned to the Americas with seventeen ships and 1,200 settlers to occupy Hispañiola where gold was found in the Americas.[237] As time went on, gold was also discovered in Puerto Rico and Cuba, resulting in the establishment of more colonies in the northern Caribbean Islands, along with the expansion of slavery among their Taino populations.

The discovery of much larger quantities of gold in Mexico in 1518 opened the floodgates for maritime expeditions to the Spanish Main. These expeditions were led by Spanish conquistadors (conquerors), who helped to colonize much of Spanish America.[238] By 1521, the Aztec empire in southern Mexico was conquered by Hernán Cortez, and by 1533 the

Inca Empire in South America was destroyed by Francisco Pizzaro. During the 1500s, Spanish convoys returning to Spain averaged sixty ships; each transporting some 200 tons of cargo that consisted mostly of gold and silver.[239]

Fig. 27: Conquistador Ponce de León Meets Puerto Rican Tainos

Spanish conquests of the Americas (including the Mayan Empire in Mexico and Guatemala)[240] led to the deaths of numerous Native Americans through foreign diseases, wars and forced labour. Spain's interests in the Spanish Caribbean naturally diminished as Spain expanded its overseas empire in the more lucrative regions of Central and South America. [241] Nevertheless, Hispañiola and Cuba continued to play a critical role in replenishing Spanish armadas travelling to and from the Spanish Main and Spain.[242]

From the mid-1500s until the late 1700s, wars between competing European states had spread to the Caribbean region.[243] Competing powers included the Spanish, English, French and Dutch states. As part of their strategy, European powers granted privateers the authority or license to attack and plunder enemy ships and territories within the Americas.[244]

The rush for gold and new territories among European powers generated an influx of Europeans that significantly increased the number of European colonies and/or expanded their territories—Spanish, Portuguese, English, French, and Dutch—throughout the Americas. Columbus' landfall on San Salvador Island had subsequently triggered the unfolding of the nations of the modern Americas at the dawning of a new era.

With the signing of peace treaties between European states and the resultant unemployment of privateers and sailors came an era of rampant piracy in the Caribbean, commonly referred to as the golden age of piracy. This infamous period lasted from around 1650 to 1730 for the pirates of the Caribbean region.[245] Many of these maritime outlaws were eventually killed, imprisoned or hung with the exception of those who were granted amnesty for giving up their nefarious trade.

The era of piracy in The Bahamas ended shortly after the arrival of Captain Woodes Rogers in 1718, the colony's first royal governor and a former privateer.[246] Captain Rogers was tasked with ridding the English colony of marauding pirates and restoring law and order throughout the colony.

The Lucayan Story

Fig. 28: Captain Woodes Rogers

A no-nonsense leader, Captain Rogers hung the last of the swashbucklers[20] who refused to give up their trade around the Lucayan islands, and chased the remaining diehard renegades out of town.[247] Governor Rogers went on to form

---

[20] Swashbuckler: a person or a character in a movie, book, etc., who is very brave and has many exciting adventures.

the first parliament and created the first coat of arms with the motto: Expulsis Piratus, Commercia Restituta (Latin for Pirates Expelled. Commerce Restored).[248] This effectively ended the taking of spoils from European ships by pirates in the Lucayan archipelago during the period of the gold rush in the Americas.

Questions

1. What drove early Europeans to focus their attention on colonizing Central and South America?

2. What are the major indigenous empires that the Spanish settlers destroyed on the American mainland?

3. What years were known as the golden age of piracy?

4. Who was Woodes Rogers?

Ch. 15 ~ Tracing Lucayan Roots

Today, the peoples of Puerto Rico, the Dominican Republic and Cuba are able to trace their genetic roots back to the Taino people who originally inhabited their islands.[249] Additionally, Arawak-speaking communities still exist in the South American countries of Venezuela, Brazil, Surinam, Guyana and Colombia.[250]

Remarkably, direct descendants of Caribs still live on the Caribbean Island of Dominica.[251] Also, the Garifuna people (or Black Caribs), who are of Carib and African descent, and were originally from Saint Vincent and the Grenadines in the eastern Caribbean, still exist.[252] Today, the Garifuna people have well established communities in Belize, Guatemala, Nicaragua and Honduras in Central America.

Their history dates back to 1797 when the British won control of Saint Vincent and the Grenadines following an uprising of the islands' Garifuna people.[253] In 1797, the last of the Garifuna people were deported by the British from their native homeland to the Spanish-controlled island of Roatán off the east coast of Honduras.

Although Arawak-speaking peoples and Caribs are still alive, and many people in Puerto Rico, the Dominican Republic and Cuba carry hereditary traits of their Taino roots[254], the Lucayans have perished without 'genetic trace.'[255] The enslavement and subsequent extinction of the native

Lucayans have made them the first indigenous people of the modern Americas to have suffered genocide at the hands of European explorers.

The fact that they were a vulnerable people made them an attractive prey for those who sought to enslave them for their personal enrichment. Consequently, the tragic demise of the original inhabitants of The Bahamas and the Turks and Caicos Islands has placed an inherent responsibility upon the modern-day inheritors of these Lucayan islands to do their part to make the world around them a more peaceful place.

Questions

1. Which of the following people are unable to trace their genetic roots: The Arawaks, The Caribs, The Tainos or the Lucayans?

2. Who were the Garifuna people and where are they now?

3. What is that 'inherent responsibility' that present-day Bahamians and Turks and Caicos Islanders were left to fulfill?

Ch. 16 ~ The Lucayan Legacy

With few artifacts and firsthand accounts upon which to build, the plight of the Lucayans has been largely overlooked in most parts of the world. Yet, telltale signs of their legacy still live on through language, food and lifestyle as evidenced through such Lucayan-Taino words as 'maize,' ' barbeque,' 'hurricane' (meaning evil spirit) [256], 'tobacco,' and 'canoe' that are commonplace in today's world.[257]

Former Lucayan sites have been discovered throughout the Lucayan archipelago.[258] Evidence of Lucayan existence is also found in the names of several of the Bahama Islands, such as (Grand) Bahama, Bimini, Exuma, Mayaguana, Samana Cay and Inagua. Additional signs are found in the names of the Turks and Caicos Islands at the southeastern end of the Lucayan chain, such as the name 'Caicos,' which is derived from a Lucayan word[259] meaning 'outer' or 'far away island'[260] or 'string of islands.'[261]

Interestingly, the life and legacy of the Lucayan people (as an indigenous people) were filled with a number of 'firsts' at the beginning of this new era in world history. The Lucayans were the first to:

- Welcome European explorers to their shores after Christopher Columbus made his first landfall in the Americas on a Lucayan island in 1492.

- Witness the birthing or the unfolding of the modern Americas.

- Experience the initial effects of the Columbian Exchange[21] that advanced globalization[22] by establishing permanent maritime trade between Europe and the Americas.[262]

- Be seen as potential slaves ('servants') among the indigenous peoples of the Americas by Columbus, which preceded the Transatlantic Slave Trade.

- Be completely stripped of their homeland by European colonizers.

- Suffer total genocide.

Ironically, the eastward migration of ancient civilization out of Asia culminated [23] with the birthing of the modern Americas juxtaposed[24] with the extinction of the Lucayan people. Various offshoots of this eastward migration had permanently settled the lands of North, Central and South

---

[21] Columbian Exchange: "...the exchange of diseases, ideas, food, crops and populations between the New World and the Old World following the voyage to the Americas by Christopher Columbus in 1492." See: The Columbian Exchange: A History of Disease, Food, and Ideas. https://www.jstor.org/stable/25703506?seq=1#page_scan_tab_contents [Retrieved: 21 August 2016].
[22] Globalization: the development of an increasingly integrated global economy marked especially by free trade, free flow of capital, and the tapping of cheaper foreign labor markets.
[23] Culminate: to reach the end or the final result of something.
[24] Juxtapose: to place (different things) together in order to create an interesting effect or to show how they are the same or different.

America, which was followed by the settling of the Caribbean Islands, and then the Lucayan Islands. The arrival of the Lucayans in the Lucayan Islands, along with their ultimate demise essentially represented the end of the road for ancient civilization's eastward trek out of Asia and the beginning of a modern journey towards globalization.[25]

Common to the experience of the indigenous peoples throughout the Americas during the post-Columbian[26] era were the atrocities of oppression, forced-starvation, murder, rape, plunder, transmission of deadly diseases, and religious tyranny by their foreign invaders.[263] The Lucayan experience was no different, with the exception that their demise gave them the undesired distinction of being the first Amerindian people to suffer the complete eradication of their race in a post-Columbian era.

Paradoxically,[27] what is known as the "rebirth"[264] of the Americas entailed a tragic death toll for many other indigenous tribes, as well as African slaves, which eventually joined the Lucayans among the ranks of enslavement and/or extinction. The Lucayans were therefore at the forefront of a number of world-changing events that occurred on or around the shores of The Bahamas and the Turks and Caicos Islands.

Thus, the Lucayan legacy is more far-reaching than what meets the eye. As the first to suffer genocide within the entire Americas at the hands of foreign invaders, the Lucayan legacy represents the plight of all Native Americans, as well as that of African slaves and their

---

[25] Globalization: the development of an increasingly integrated global economy marked especially by free trade, free flow of capital, and the tapping of cheaper foreign labor markets.
[26] Post-Columbian: After Christopher Columbus.
[27] Paradoxical: not being the normal or usual kind

descendants who were later imported to the Americas, and all other peoples of the modern world who have suffered (or are suffering) a similar fate. Consequently, the history, heritage and legacy of the Lucayans are just as much a part of the entire Americas as it is The Bahamas' and the Turks and Caicos Islands.' Through the Lucayan story, we are made aware of:

- The sufferings of the indigenous, as well as other oppressed (or defenseless) peoples of the Americas and the world.

- How humanity's unrestrained quest for power, wealth, and pleasure will inevitably[28] lead to the demise of peoples and nations, if left unchecked.

- The need to promote freedom, justice and peace for the long term, sustainable development of communities and nations.

- An inherent responsibility for the modern-day inheritors and successors of The Bahamas and the Turks and Caicos Islands to lead the way in fostering the virtues of peace, in view of the trauma and tragedy that originated from these shores.

Spanish Conquistadors (Conquerors) and other Europeans were driven to raid and plunder the New World, because their unrestrained quest for power, wealth, and pleasure took priority over the need for freedom, justice and peace.

---

[28] Inevitably: as is to be expected. http://www.merriam-webster.com/dictionary/ineveitably

Interestingly, almost 500 years later, the importance of freedom, justice and peace for the preservation of humanity was expressed in the preamble of the United Nations Universal Declaration of Human Rights.[265] The Declaration was adopted in 1948, three years after World War II ended. Approximately 60 million lives were lost during this war due to the unrestrained drive for power, wealth and pleasure by Adolph Hitler, the head of Nazi Germany, and his allies.

Freedom[29] permits individuals and nations to do their part to make the world a better place. Justice[30] preserves freedom by ensuring that necessary laws, policies and practices are in place for the protection of society and the betterment of nations. Peace[31] is the state in which all concerned are systematically[32] benefitted by the rewards of honest work, equal opportunity to succeed, physical safety and social order as they go about making the world around them a better place.

The awareness of the Lucayan story should therefore encourage modern-day inhabitants of these Lucayan islands (and those who visit them) to bring about real change by learning from the mistakes of the past, improving upon the positive accomplishments of others, and creating success stories of their own as they do their part to make the world around them a more peaceful place.

---

[29] Freedom: ability to move or act as desired.
[30] Justice: the process or result of using laws to fairly judge and punish crimes and criminals
[31] Peace: a state or period of mutual concord between governments; a pact or agreement to end hostilities between those who have been at war or in a state of enmity; a state of security or order within a community provided for by law or custom; harmony in personal relations
[32] Systematically: using a careful system or method: done according to a system

Questions

1. List three things that the Lucayans were the first to do or to experience during or shortly after Columbus' first landfall?

2. List three things that the Lucayan story makes humanity aware of?

3. What is the cause of wars and conflicts and how can they be prevented?

Ch. 17 ~ The Lucayan Sea

"I knew it! The waters in The Bahamas are as beautiful on Earth as they are from space!"[266]
Retired American astronaut and former Commander of the International Space Station, Scott Kelly while in The Bahamas on 8 August 2016.

It was not until after Columbus made his first landfall in the Americas on San Salvador Island in the Lucayan chain that news of a New World began to spread throughout Spain and the rest of Europe. Occurring at the threshold of the modern era, this historic event ultimately resulted in the unfolding of the modern nations of the Americas. In fact, the preamble to The Bahamas' constitution describes Columbus' rediscovery of these islands as heralding the 'rebirth' of the New World. [267]

Consequently, the modern nations of the Americas that exist today were spawned from the geographical womb of the Lucayan Islands. In essence, the unintended arrival of European explorers in the New World at the onset of a new era in modern history gave The Bahamas and the Turks and Caicos Islands the distinction of being the geographical birthplace of the modern Americas.[268]

Essential to this birthing process were the glistening waters surrounding the Lucayan islands, which became a veritable[33] aquatic[34] highway facilitating easy transport to the Americas by Europeans. These waters were the setting where civilizations from major continental landmasses of the world were permanently reunited. As the birthplace of the modern Americas, the waters surrounding The Bahamas and the Turks and Caicos Islands indeed have a story to tell. It is a story whose inception is marred with tragedy and trauma, yet whose end inspires and facilitates hope and peace.

For the purpose of this book, the Lucayan Sea[269] refers to the waters that surround The Bahamas and the Turks and Caicos Islands or the Lucayan archipelago.[270] In more modern times, these waters extend seaward (or outwards) from the coasts of The Bahamas and the Turks and Caicos Islands to the outer limits of their respective territorial, contiguous [35] or exclusive economic maritime zones. According to the United Nations Convention on the Law of the Sea, national waters can extend from 12 to 200 nautical miles outwards from the coast or from the baseline that is drawn around an archipelago.[271]

Left in the wake of the Lucayan demise are the tranquil yet vibrant waters that surround The Bahamas and the Turks and Caicos Islands. Having borne witness to the life and legacy of the Lucayans, these tropical waters appear to be endowed with a natural ability to tell the Lucayan story, having been blessed with the deep underwater canyon known as the Tongue of the Ocean.

---

[33] Veritable: true or real.
[34] Aquatic: done in or on water.
[35] Contiguous: used to describe things that touch each other or are immediately next to each other.

The Lucayan Story

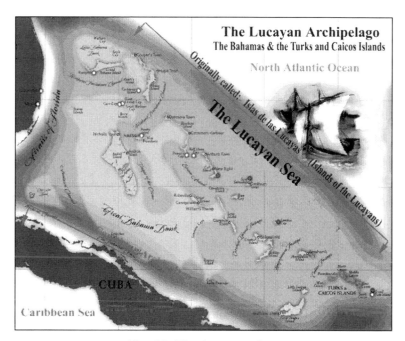

Fig. 29: The Lucayan Sea

Adorned with a seemingly endless assortment of lucid[36] blue hues, these waters of The Bahamas and the Turks and Caicos Islands boast a sublime[37] clarity for which most heavenly hideaways could only wish. Warm, temperate[38] seas change from crystal-clear to a rich emerald near sandy shores; and from a mesmerizing[39] turquoise to the deepest of sapphire and cobalt-blue in a matter of feet near the ocean's edge.

---

[36] Lucid: very clear and easy to understand.
[37] Sublime: very beautiful or good: causing strong feelings of admiration or wonder.
[38] Temperate: having temperatures that are not too hot or too cold.
[39] Mesmerize: to interest or amaze (someone) so much that nothing else is seen or noticed.

The shallow waters of these islands provide a sneak peek at the kaleidoscopic[40] coral and tropical utopia[41] at one's feet. In deeper waters, blue shades hint at the underwater world below—a world that extends to a depth of some 8,000 feet (2,438 m) beneath the surface. Furthermore, coming to grips with this underwater world is of little difficulty considering these are undoubtedly some of the clearest waters on the planet, boasting visibility up to an incredible 200 feet (61 m). These waters contain almost five percent of the Earth's coral reefs.[272] Viewed from space, their beauty has been extolled in a poem written by the veteran astronaut, Story Musgrave, entitled "Oh Bahamas."[273]

Staring into these waters, it is hard to imagine the enslavement and genocide that once unfolded from these shores. Regrettably, the Lucayan story is reminiscent of the pain and suffering that have repeatedly occurred throughout the course of human history. Nevertheless, the waters that surround these islands and the story they tell are a rare maritime treasure that beckons modern-day inheritors and visitors alike to do their part to make the world a better place.

The rich heritage and legacy of these islands might very well qualify their surrounding waters as a World Heritage Site by the United Nations Educational, Scientific and Cultural Organization (UNESCO).[274] Being designated a World Heritage Site would therefore be another impactful way of keeping the history and heritage of The Bahama and the Turks and Caicos Islands alive.

Unlike the American continents whose national borders are geographically connected or the islands of the Caribbean

---

[40] Kaleidoscopic: a changing pattern or scene.
[41] Utopia: an imaginary place in which the government, laws, and social conditions are perfect.

that share a common sea (that is, the Caribbean Sea, which derived its name from the name of the Caribs), the Lucayan chain of islands does not share a single landmass or body of water under a common name that distinguishes them as a unified group of islands. The idea of naming the historic waters of The Bahamas and the Turks and Caicos Islands after the Lucayans would therefore create a shared identity for the two groups of territories within the archipelago, in addition to promoting their common history, geography, and culture.

To name these waters after the Lucayans would therefore be a fitting way to pay lasting tribute to the life, plight and legacy of the indigenous Lucayans. Such a tribute would also act as a permanent reminder of the rare heritage that these islands possess, and would be symbolic of the following:

- The end of the eastward trek of ancient civilization in its quest for a better life with the arrival of the Lucayans in The Bahamas and the Turks and Caicos Islands.

- The permanent 'reunion' of civilizations through maritime travel and trade after Columbus made his first landfall on an island in the Lucayan chain.

- The birthplace of the modern Americas from which the modern nations unfolded at the beginning of modern history.

- The peaceful Lucayans, who were the first indigenous people to suffer genocide within the modern Americas after being forcibly removed from their homeland and later died under the abuses of slavery.

- The need to promote freedom, justice, and peace for the preservation of humanity in light of the Lucayan demise.

- The need to foster personal health, environmental integrity, and caring for each other for the promotion of peace.

- The vulnerability of island people. The name 'Lucayan' means, 'Island People.' Island people are vulnerable[42] people. Like the Lucayans, today's inhabitants of these islands are equally vulnerable to threats of violence, economic plunder, and environmental disasters, and should therefore do their part to promote peace in light of the Lucayan story.

- An inherent appeal that emanates from the shores of The Bahamas and the Turks and Caicos Islands for those who inhabit these islands (and those who visit them) to do their part to make the world a better place as ambassadors of peace.

To give these waters a name that befit the heritage of these islands and the legacy of the people, who once inhabited them, will naturally promote the cause for peace, and thus hope for a better world.

---

[42] Vulnerable: open to attack, harm, or damage

The Lucayan Story

In view of the Lucayan genocide, and the significance of world-changing events the Lucayans had witnessed around their shores, what could be a more fitting tribute to the life and legacy of the Lucayans than dedicating the surrounding waters to their lasting memory?

Questions

1. What makes The Bahamas and the Turks and Caicos Islands the 'birthplace of the modern Americas?'

2. Which indigenous people was the Caribbean Sea named after?

3. List three things that the waters surrounding The Bahamas and the Turks and Caicos Islands are symbolic of?

Ch. 18 ~ How the Oceans of the Americas got their Names

The names, Atlantic Ocean, Pacific Ocean, and Caribbean Sea are not indigenous or native to the Americas—they are mainly due to European influence, During the early years of Spanish exploration, the New World was officially dubbed, "Islas y Tierra Firme" in Spanish or 'Islands and Mainland' in English. 'Islas,' meaning 'Islands,' came to represent the islands of the West Indies and "Tierra Firme" meaning 'Mainland,' initially referred to the north coast of South America. The New World was also called, "the Islands and Mainland of the Indies in the Ocean Sea."[275]

For two decades after European arrival, the Atlantic Ocean and the Caribbean Sea were considered one ocean and were called the 'Ocean Sea,' and not the 'Atlantic Ocean.'[276] Nevertheless, early European explorers were responsible for giving the ocean around the eastern seaboard of the Americas and the sea within the Caribbean the names that are currently used today.

The ocean on the eastern seaboard of the Americas (or what is now known as the western Atlantic from Canada to southern Argentina) was initially given the Spanish name, 'Mar Del Norte' (the 'Sea of the North' or 'North Sea') and not the 'Atlantic Ocean.' The ocean on the western seaboard of the Americas (or the eastern Pacific Ocean) was initially called, 'Mar del Sur,' [277] (meaning 'Sea of the South' or 'South Sea')—a name given it by Spanish explorer Vasco Nuñez de Balbóa. The name 'Mar del Sur' distinguished it from Mar del Norte, which was north of the Isthmus of Panama (a narrow strip of land in Panama that joins South America with Costa Rica in Central America). Balbóa had crossed the Isthmus of Panama in September 1513.[278] He led an expedition that made him the first European to see the Ocean.

However, the Pacific Ocean would get its permanent name from the Portuguese explorer, Ferdinand Magellan, who was the first European to sail across the ocean in 1520. Magellan named the ocean 'Mar Pacifico' meaning 'Peaceful Sea.'[43] The first map of the Pacific Ocean and Mar del Sur was published by Flemish cartographer, Abraham Ortelius, in 1589.[44] The name Mar del Sur was later replaced by the name, Pacific Ocean.

Mar del Norte ('North Sea') later became known as the 'Atlantic Ocean.' The etymology [45] of the name Atlantic Ocean is still debated. However, it is generally believed that the name was derived from the fabled[46] Greek god, Titan, who was made to bear the heavens on his shoulders as a form of punishment. The name 'Atlantic' is also said to be derived from the Atlas Mountains in northwest Africa, and was later applied to the waters off the coast of northern Africa. Eventually the name 'Atlantic Ocean' included the entire ocean between the Americas, and Africa and

---

[43] http://blog.oxforddictionaries.com/2015/06/water-water-everywhere-ocean-names/
[44] See:
https://en.wikipedia.org/wiki/Pacific_Ocean#European_exploration
[45] Etymology: an explanation of where a word came from : the history of a word.
[46] Fabled: told about in old stories: the history of a word.

Europe.[279] Consequently, the name is not indigenous to Americas or The Bahamas and the Turks and Caicos Islands.

The Caribbean Sea was also known as Mar del Norte ('North Sea') before the name 'Atlantic Ocean' was applied to the eastern seaboard of the Americas. The Caribbean Sea was among the last bodies of water near the Spanish Main to be given a distinct identity. Lopez de Valesco proposed that the Caribbean Sea be named the Gulf of the Canibales (Canibales is the Spanish word for cannibals),[280] which was a name imposed on the war-faring Caribs, who were presumed to be cannibals.[281]

Additionally, Valesco had distinguished the Caribbean Sea from the Gulf of Mexico. However, it was Thomas Jefferys who acknowledged in his West Indies Atlas (1773) that the waters to the south and west of the Caribbean Islands were "sometimes called the Caribbean-Sea, which name it would be better to adopt, than to leave this space quite anonymous."[282] However, the historic waters of the Lucayan archipelago that gave birth to the nations of the modern Americas, and witnessed the demise of the first indigenous people at the beginning of a new era for the Americas were never named.

Questions

1. What was the northern coastal area of South America originally called by early Spanish explorers?

2. What were the original names given the Atlantic and Pacific Oceans?

3. What was one of the last bodies of waters to be given a permanent name in the Americas?

Ch. 19 ~ Ambassadors of Peace

Lamentably, what the Lucayans thought was a peaceful end to an ancient journey would quickly culminate in their demise with the landfall of Columbus on their shores. The tragic end of the Lucayans distinguished these original inhabitants of The Bahamas and the Turks and Caicos Islands as the first indigenous people of the modern Americas to suffer total genocide. Consequently, the extinction of the peaceful Lucayans carries with it an 'inherent responsibility' for the people of these islands to do their part to make the world around them a more peaceful place. This priceless responsibility is directly related to a compelling[47] identity[48] for the inheritors of these Lucayan Islands.

Today, many struggle to define who they are as individuals and as a people.[283] Now at the beginning of a new era of existence, which is the second 40-year period of political and social change since 1973,[284] a new opportunity has opened up for the successors of these islands to rediscover who they are as a people, and the purpose they were meant

---

[47] Compelling: strong and forceful: causing you to feel that you must do something.
[48] Identity: strong and forceful: the set of qualities and beliefs that make one person or group different from others: Individuality

to fulfill in order to make their world a better place. The history, geography and culture of these islands contain all-important clues that point to a hidden identity for the people of these islands as 'ambassadors of peace.' Interestingly, the original inhabitants of these islands, the Lucayans, were the first ambassadors of peace, who welcomed Columbus and his men to their shores.

In the case of The Bahamas and to some extent, the Turks and Caicos Islands, the people who inhabited these islands after the Lucayan demise made relatively peaceful transitions from colonialism through slavery, racism, the achievement of political leadership by a 'black majority'—once ruled for many years by a 'white minority' government—and the eventual attainment of independence from Great Britain—a historical event that was described as a "quiet revolution" and "hailed as a model of democracy for all emerging nations of the world" by Juan Tripp, the founder of Pan American Airlines.[285] Even today, the inhabitants of these islands are known to be a traditionally peaceful people. These, and much more, all shed light on the unique identity that the people of these islands were meant to have as 'ambassadors of peace.'

Building on this unique identity is the importance of freedom, justice and peace that are transmitted throughout the Lucayan story. History has proven that these higher ideals are vital for the preservation of humanity. In their absence, the pursuit of power, wealth, and pleasure takes priority. Left unchecked, this pursuit would often degenerate[49] into acts of oppression, injustice and despair with the destruction (or extinction) of humanity being its end result. Consequently, freedom, justice and peace are

---

[49] Degenerates; having sunk to a condition below that which is normal to a type; especially: having sunk to a lower and usually corrupt and vicious state.

fundamental to achieving the long term, sustainable development of human life. In understanding and appreciating this identity as ambassadors of peace, Bahamians and Turks and Caicos islanders will be better positioned to do their part in making the world a better place.

National identity [50] therefore involves a people knowing 'who' they are in relation to a higher ideal. In other words, a national belief in (or submission to) freedom, justice or peace produces an enduring commitment to the fulfillment of that ideal, thus enhancing the chances of preserving a community, nation or humanity itself.

National identity not only involves 'knowing who you are,' but also includes the fulfillment of purpose [51] or 'why' a people or nation exists. In other words, purpose involves knowing the problems that a people was destined to solve in relation to a particular ideal. For example, a nation that believes in freedom, justice or peace would—at least, to some extent—seek to solve those problems that would prevent freedom, justice or peace from being experienced politically, economically, socially, environmentally, and so on. But to do so, such a people, will need to develop the necessary skills and character.

According to the Bradley Project—a study on America's national identity—Americans define their identity as a 'commitment to freedom.' Fundamental to America's commitment to freedom is her belief in 'free speech, freedom of religion, freedom of opportunity and political

---

[50] Identity: the qualities, beliefs, etc., that make a particular person or group different from others.
[51] Purpose: the reason why something is done or used: the aim or intention of something.

freedom.'[286] Freedom; in essence, is the American Dream that Americans would live for, and if necessary, die for. Consequently, the unique cultural expression of Americans (or the American Way) is seen as Americans go about their daily lives solving problems and meeting needs related to their commitment to freedom. America's belief in freedom, for example, became evident during World War II when over 400,000 American lives were lost as America stood in defense of freedom.[287] National identity therefore goes beyond language, food, music, arts, festivals, sports, architecture, and other cultural[52] activities that are unique to a people.[288] These are but expressions of the unique way a people live as a result of their identity.

The people of these Lucayan islands are traditionally a peaceful people, who overcame the oppression and racial divide of the past. Their leading industry (tourism)[289] was founded upon their world-renowned hospitality,[290] and the naturally peaceful settings these islands offer. [291] Consequently, the history, geography and culture of these Lucayan islands and their people appear to unveil an identity and a purpose[292] for today's inhabitants of these islands as 'ambassadors of peace.'[293]

Coincidentally, on the eve of its second 40-year period of political and social change, The Bahamas celebrated its 41st Independence Anniversary under the theme: Celebrating Our Culture: A Commitment to Peace. That evening, The Bahamas broke the Guinness World Record for 'the most people blowing conch shells' as "a call for peace to the nations of the world from the Islands of The Bahamas."[294]

In accepting an identity as ambassadors of peace, the people of The Bahamas and the Turks and Caicos Islands

---

[52] Cultural: of or relating to a particular group of people and their habits, beliefs, traditions, etc.

The Lucayan Story

have also accepted that 'inherent responsibility' to do their part to make the world a more peaceful place in light of the Lucayan genocide. With this calling also comes a corresponding vision and a commitment to do those things (regardless of how big or small) that foster and promote the virtues (or values) of peace. Among these virtues is the promoting of personal health, environmental integrity, and caring for each other during everyday living. Hence, ambassadors of peace are committed to drawing upon the virtues of their islands' heritage to create a peace-filled world, while encouraging others to do the same in memory of a tragic past.

Ironically, Columbus' historic landfall made these islands the birthplace of the modern Americas—a type of 'motherland' for the modern Americas. Mothers are leaders in their own right, who influence their offspring with vision for a better world, integrity for the sustainment of that world, and purpose for solving problems to make that vision for a better world a reality.

The people of The Bahamas and the Turks and Caicos Islands were therefore destined to be leaders, who inspire others throughout the Americas and the modern world to do their part as sowers of peace in this world. By so doing, they make judicious[53] use of the birthright[54] which they have been given. Moreover, the people of these Lucayan Islands were graced with every provision to fulfill their calling as ambassadors of peace.

An example of this calling was clearly seen when member states of the Commonwealth Heads of Government Meeting

---

[53] Judicious: having or showing good judgment
[54] Birthright: a right that you have because you were born into a particular position, family, place, etc., or because it is a right of all people

held in Nassau, Bahamas, in 1985 agreed under the leadership of the then Bahamas Prime Minister, Sir Lynden Pindling, to press for continued sanctions against South Africa's apartheid [55] government during their Nassau Accord.[295] This decision later contributed to the late Nelson Mandela being freed in 1990 after 27 years of imprisonment. In 1993, Mr. Mandela became the first black president of South Africa. He later visited the Bahamas before and during his presidency where he paid courtesy calls upon former Prime Ministers Hubert Ingraham and Sir Lynden Pindling, and his wife, Dame Marguerite Pindling (later appointed Governor General of The Commonwealth of The Bahamas on 8 July 2014). During his visit, Mr. Mandela thanked the people of The Bahamas for their stance against apartheid. [296]

More than five centuries have passed since the Lucayan genocide has taken place, yet the world continues on its quest for peace while caught in a web of strife and unrest that could once again threaten the peace and security of these Lucayan Islands. Millions now converge each year on the tropical shores of The Bahamas and the Turks and Caicos Islands in pursuit of that peace. Today, the inhabitants and visitors of these collective islands now stand at the crossroads of a new era with an unprecedented opportunity to both foster [56] and host their calling as ambassadors of peace for the making of a better world.

---

[55] Apartheid: a former policy of segregation and political and economic discrimination against non-European groups in the Republic of South Africa

[56] Foster: to help (something) grow or develop

Questions

1. What is that 'inherent responsibility' that the people of these islands have been called to fulfill in light of the Lucayan genocide?

2. What is the difference between 'identity' and 'purpose'?

3. List three 'peaceful' transitions made by Bahamians from the time of the Lucayan extinction to Independence?

Ch. 20 ~ Discovery Day

The unrestrained quest for power, wealth, and pleasure did not achieve the end result intended by the colonial powers of yesteryears. These empires have since dwindled into much smaller nation-states challenged by political, economic and social challenges. The Lucayan story, in its own small way, rediscovers the underlying causes of humanity's failure to achieve a better life, and presents a renewed appreciation for the higher ideals of freedom, justice and peace.

It is interesting to note that October 12 marks the day when Columbus first encountered the Lucayans during his first landfall in the Americas on San Salvador Island in the Lucayan chain. Since 1926, The Bahamas has observed this day as 'Discovery Day' when Watling's Island was renamed San Salvador.[297] October 12 is also traditionally observed as Columbus Day in a number of countries in the Americas, including the United States.

The Bahamas Government, however, has replaced the Discovery Day holiday with 'National Heroes Day' for the purpose of honoring the national heroes of The Bahamas. (National Heroes Day in the Turks and Caicos Islands is celebrated in May). Consequently, Discovery Day is only observed annually, and not celebrated in the traditional sense as of 12 October 2013.[298] The Turks and Caicos

Islands have also changed their Columbus Day event to National Heritage Day, which is celebrated as a holiday.[299]

Nevertheless, both names for this historic event are appropriate; they work hand-in-hand. The word 'discovery' means: 'the act of finding or learning something for the first time.[57] Its root meaning implies: to take away or apart; to remove the cover or to reveal that which is hidden.[58] Consequently, Bahamians and Turks and Caicos Islanders should seek to uncover the truth (Discovery Day) about humanity's quest for a better life as revealed through their heritage (National Heritage Day), and to celebrate those heroes who promote the cause of freedom, justice and/or peace (National Heroes Day).

The Lucayan Story also proposes a role that the people of The Bahamas and the Turks and Caicos Islands ought to play as ambassadors of peace in helping to make the world a better place. Interestingly, the peaceful ambience created by the natural beauty and hospitality of the Bahamian people helped Dr. Martin Luther King to write his acceptance speech for the Nobel Peace Prize in 1964 after visiting Bimini Island.[300] The Bahamas was also the site for the pressing of sanctions that led, in part, to the freedom of Mandela.[301] The peaceful nature of these islands and their people has therefore produced heroes, who, at one time or another, did their part to make the world a better place.

Although Discovery Day or National Heritage Day is no longer celebrated in the traditional sense of observing Columbus' first landfall in the Americas, the events could be set aside by the people of these Lucayan Islands as a day

---

[57] Discovery: the act of finding or learning something for the first time: the act of discovering something.
[58] http://www.etymonline.com/index.php?term=dis-&allowed_in_frame=0

for promoting the virtues of peace in view of the Lucayan story. In promoting these virtues, the inhabitants of these islands would seek to learn from the mistakes of the past, improve on the positive accomplishments made by others, and create success stories of their own to make the world a better place.

Appendix ~ Lucayan and Taino Timelines

Circa

A.D. 600: The Tainos begin to settle islands in the southern Lucayan chain.

710: Arabs and Berbers (North Africans) invade the Iberian Peninsula (Spain).

1250: The Tainos arrive in Cuba.

3 August, 1492: Christopher Columbus departs Palos, Spain for the East Indies by sailing west.

12 October, 1492: Spain regains control of Iberian Peninsula from Muslim Moors to reunite Spain. Christopher Columbus makes landfall in the Americas on a tiny island (Guanahani) in the Lucayan chain, which he renamed San Salvador.

26 October, 1492: Columbus arrives off Cuba.

5 December, 1492: Columbus arrives at Hispañiola. He is welcomed by the Taino and is informed of gold on the island.

16 January, 1493: Columbus departs Hispañiola for Spain; leaving 39 of his men behind to construct a fort and to look for gold at a site he named La Navidad (in modern day Haiti) on the north coast of Hispañiola.

15 March, 1493: Columbus returns to Palos, Spain, ending his first voyage to the Americas.

May, 1493: Pope Alexander VI confirms a demarcation (maritime boundary) line for the purpose of establishing ownership of lands and territories discovered by Spain and Portugal. The demarcation line was initially 100 leagues west of the Cape Verde Isles in the Atlantic Ocean. All lands and territories to the west of this vertical line belonged to Spain and all lands and territories to the east of it belonged to Portugal.

1493: Columbus departs Cadiz, Spain on his second voyage to the Americas with a fleet of 17 ships and 1,500 men with intent to colonize the islands.

19 November, 1493: Columbus discovers Puerto Rico. Taino Indians show Columbus gold in the rivers.

22 November, 1493: Columbus arrives at Hispañiola. Enslavement of the Tainos begins later that year.

28 November, 1493: Columbus returns to La Navidad in Hispañiola and discovers the fort destroyed. All European occupants left behind during Columbus' first voyage were killed by the Tainos.

8 December, 1493: Columbus establishes colony at La Isabela in Hispañiola.

1493 to 1500s: Native Americans die from European diseases.

30 April, 1494: Columbus arrives at Cuba.

5 May, 1494: Columbus arrives at Jamaica.

14 May, 1494: Columbus returns to Cuba.

June, 1494: The Line of Demarcation is moved 370 leagues west of Cape Verde Isles under the Treaty of Tordesillas.

20 August, 1494: Columbus returns to Hispañiola.

10 March, 1496: Columbus departs Hispañiola for Spain.

8 June, 1496: Columbus arrives at Portugal, ending his second voyage to the Americas.

30 May, 1498: Columbus departs Sanlucar, Spain with six ships on his third voyage to the Americas.

31 July, 1498: Columbus arrives at Trinidad in the southern Caribbean chain.

19 August, 1498: Columbus arrives at Hispañiola.

1499: Italian explorer, Amerigo Vespucci, captures 232 Lucayans as slaves from the Lucayan archipelago.

October, 1500: Columbus is sent back to Spain under arrest and in chains, ending his third voyage to the Americas.

1502: African slaves imported into the Americas (Hispañiola).

11 May, 1502: Columbus departs Cadiz, Spain with four ships for his fourth and final voyage to the Americas.

29 June, 1502: Columbus arrives at Santo Domingo on the south coast of Hispañiola, Spain.

30 July, 1502: Columbus arrives at the Mosquito Coast in Central America (now modern-day Nicaragua).

25 June, 1503: Columbus and crew marooned at Jamaica.

29 June, 1504: Columbus and crew rescued from Jamaica and return to Hispañiola.

11 July, 1504: Columbus departs Hispañiola for Spain.

20 May, 1506: Columbus dies at Valladolid, Spain.

1508: Ponce de León establishes first settlement in Puerto Rico.

1509: Diego Cólon (Columbus' son) becomes governor of Hispañiola and expresses his displeasure with the performance of Native American slaves.

1509: King Ferdinand of Spain authorizes the enslavement of indigenous peoples from the neighboring islands of Hispañiola.

1509: Ponce de León begins conquest of Puerto Rico.

1509: Spanish settle Jamaica.

22 January, 1510: African slaves systematically shipped to the Americas (Hispañiola).

1511: Diego Colon settles Cuba. Havana is founded. Taino in Puerto Rico revolt against the Spanish.

12 February, 1512: Taino Chief, Hatuey, is burned at the stake in Cuba.

1512: First African slaves imported into Cuba from Hispañiola.

1513: The Tainos were required to willfully submit to Spanish authority under threat of slavery, loss of property or even death.

2 April, 1513: Spanish explorer, Ponce de León makes landfall in Florida.

1514: Spanish crown authorized Spanish settlers to marry the Tainos.

1514: Conquistador Hernán Cortés sets sail from Cuba to conquer Mexico. Cortés' success results in Havana, Cuba becoming a transit port for Spanish ships returning to Spain from the American mainland (or Spanish Main).

1520: The Lucayan islands are depopulated of native Lucayans.

1524: African slaves shipped to work in Cuban gold mines.

1530: Spanish settle Trinidad.

By 1535: Taino culture in Hispañiola is destroyed by the Spanish.

1537: Pope Paul III issues a decree, called "Sublimus Deus." The decree opposes the enslavement of Native Americans and recognizes the indigenous peoples as "true men." This decree, however, was bypassed by Conquistadors and colonists by paying tribute to Spanish monarchs using profits from forced labor (Encomienda) or by instituting forced labor (Repartimiento) or through land grants (Hacienda and Rancho).

1570: Gold mines in Puerto Rico were declared empty.

1600: King Philip III of Spain outlaws enslavement of Native Americans in Spanish colonies.

23 November, 1614: Bermuda becomes a British Colony.

1648: The Bahamas is settled by Bermudian colonists of British descent.

1629: The Bahama Islands are granted to Attorney General, Sir Robert Heath, by King Charles I of England. However, no efforts to colonize these islands were made.

1660s/1670s: Bermudians begin to arrive in the Turks and Caicos Islands to collect and sell salt on a seasonal basis.

1764: The British Crown claims ownership of the Turks and Caicos Islands.

1766: The British Crown places the Turks and Caicos Islands under The Bahamas' jurisdiction.

1799: Britain grants the Bahama colony jurisdiction over the Turks and Caicos Islands.

1780s: Many American colonists loyal to the British Crown move to The Bahamas and the Turks and Caicos Islands as a result of the War of Independence between American colonists and Britain. The American loyalists also bring their African slaves with them.

Bibliography

Aceto, Michael and Williams, Jeffrey Payne. Eds. (2003). Contact Englishes of the Eastern Caribbean. Amsterdam: John Benjamin Publishing Company.

Albury, Paul. (1975) The Story of The Bahamas. London: MacMillan Caribbean.

Allsopp, Richard and Allsopp, Jeannette.(2003). Dictionary of Caribbean English Usage. Kingston, Jamaica: University of the West Indies Press.

Andrea, Alfred and Overfield, James. (2011). The Human Record: Sources of Global History, Volume I: To 1500. Boston: Cengage Learning.

Atkinson, Lesley-Gail. (Ed.). (2006).The Earliest Inhabitants: The Dynamics of the Jamaican Taíno. Kingston, Jamaica: University of the West Indies Press.

Aufderheide, Arthur C.; Rodríguez-Martín, Conrado; and Langsjoen, Odin 1998).The Cambridge encyclopedia of human paleopathology. Cambridge: Cambridge University Press.

Barratt, Peter. (2011). Bahama Saga: The epic saga of the Bahama Islands. Indiana: 1stBooks.

Barreiro, José. (1989). Indians in Cuba. Punta Maisi, Cuba: Cultural Survival Quarterly, vol. 13, no. 3.

Bodmer, Beatriz Pastor (1992). The Armature of Conquest: Spanish Accounts of the Discovery of America, 1492 – 1589. California: Stanford University Press.

Boucher, Philip P. (1992). Cannibal Encounters: Europeans and Island Caribs,1492–1763. Maryland: John Hopkins University.

Bradley, Bruce and Stanford, Dennis (2004).The North Atlantic ice-edge corridor: a possible Palaeolithic route to the New World. World Archaeology, 36(4):459-478.

Brown, Isabel Zakrzewski. (1999). Culture and Customs of the Dominican Republic. Connecticut: Greenwood Press, p.73.

Brown, Keith and Ogilvie, Sarah. (2009). Concise Encyclopedia of Languages of the World. Oxford: Elsevier Ltd., p.59.

Burke, Peter. (2008). What is Cultural History? Cambridge: Polity.

Cadigan, Sean Thomas (2009). Newfoundland and Labrador: A History Toronto: University of Toronto Press Inc.

Case, Jay Riley. (2012). An Unpredictable Gospel: American Evangelicals and World Christianity, 1812-1920. Oxford: Oxford University Press.

Castro, Daniel. (2007). Another Face of Empire: Bartolomé de Las Casas, Indigenous Rights, and Ecclesiastical Imperialism. North Carolina: Duke University Press.

Cleare, Angela, B. (2007). History of Tourism in The Bahamas: A Global Perspective. Indiana: Xlibris Corp.

Cohen, Andrew. (2007). The Unfinished Canadian: The People We Are. Toronto: McClelland & Stewart.

Columbus, Christopher and Bartolomé de las Casas. (1991). First Voyage to America: From the Log of the "Santa Maria." Toronto: Dover Publications, Inc.

Courtz, Henk (2008). A Carib Grammar and Dictionary. Toronto: Magoria Books.

Craton, Michael and Saunders, Gail. (1999). Islanders in the Stream: A History of the Bahamian People: Volume One: From Aboriginal Times to the End of Slavery. Athens, Georgia: The university of Georgia Press.

Cummins, John (1992). Columbus: Columbus' Own Journal of Discovery (newly restored and translated). New York: St. Martin's Press.

Curet, Antonio L. and Hauser, Mark W. (Ed.) (2011).Islands at the Crossroads: Migration, Seafaring, and Interaction in the Caribbean. Alabama: The University of Alabama Press

Dunn, Oliver and Kelly, James E. (Eds.). (1991). The Diario of Christopher Columbus's First Voyage to America, 1492-1493. Oklahoma: University of Oklahoma Press.

Dupuch, Etienne, Jr. (1992). Bahamas Handbook and Businessman's Annual. Nassau: E. Dupuch, Jr., Publications.

Dupuch, Etienne Jr. (2003) Bahamas Handbook. Nassau:Etienne Dupuch Jr. Publications.

Ferguson, Moira (1994). Jamaica Kincaid: Where the Land Meets the Body. Virginia: University Press of Virginia.

Fernández-Armesto,Felipe.(2008). Columbus on Himself. Indiana: Hackett Publishing, Inc.

Figueredo, D. H. and Argote-Freyre, Frank.(2008). A Brief History of the Caribbean. New York: Facts on File, Inc.

Forte, Maximilian C. (Ed.) (2006) Indigenous Resurgence in the Contemporary Caribbean: Amerindian Survival and Revival. New York: Peter Lang Publishing.

Funk, Wilfred. (1998). Word Origins: An Exploration and History of Words and Language. New York: Wings Books.

Granberry, Julian and Vescelius, Gary S. (2004).Languages of the Pre-Columbian Antilles. Alabama: The University of Alabama Press.

Hellriegel, Don and Slocum, John. (2011). Organizational Behavior. Connecticut: Cengage Learning, Inc.

Higman, B. W. (2011) A Concise History of the Caribbean. New York: Cambridge University Press.

Hulme, Peter. (1992). Colonial Encounters: Europe and the native Caribbean, 1492-1797. London: Routledge.

Jain, Jitendra. (2007). Tracing the Origin and Exploring the Causes and Consequences of Globalization. Norderstedt, Germany: Druck und Bindung—Books on Demand, GmbH.

Johnson, Doris, L. (1972). The Quiet Revolution in The Bahamas. Nassau, Bahamas: Family Islands Press.

Johnson, Whittington Bernard. (2000) Race Relations in the Bahamas, 1784-1834: The Nonviolent Transformation from a Slave to a Free Society. Arkansas: University of Arkansas Press.

Joseph, Frank and Sitchin, Zecharia. (Eds.) (2006). Discovering the Mysteries of Ancient America: Lost History and Legends Unearthed and Explored. Career Press.

Keegan, William F. (1992). The People Who Discovered Columbus: The Prehistory of The Bahamas. Florida: University Press of Florida.

Keegan, William F. and Carlson, Lisabeth A. (2008) Talking Taino: Caribbean Natural History from a Native Perspective. The University of Alabama Press, Alabama.

Klein, Herbert S. (2010). The Atlantic Slave Trade. New York: Cambridge University Press.

Kotz, Nick. (2005). Judgment Days: Lyndon Baines Johnson, Rev. Dr. Martin Luther King, Jr., and the Laws that changed America. New York: Mariner Books.

Loven, Sven. (2010). Origins of the Tainan Culture, West Indies. Alabama: University of Alabama Press.

Markham, Clements R. (Ed.). (2010). Letters of Amerigo Vespucci, and Other Documents Illustrative of His Career. New York: Cambridge University Press.

Masur, Louis P. (ed.) (1999). The Challenge of American History. Maryland: John Hopkins University Press.

McCartney, Donald M. (2004). Bahamian Culture and Factors which Impact Upon it: A Compilation of Two Essays. Pennsylvania: Dorrance Publishing Company, Inc.

McKinnen, Daniel. (1804). A Tour Through the British West Indies, in the Years 1802 and 1803, Giving a Particular Account of The Bahama Islands. London: Taylor Black-Horse Court.

McMorran, Jennifer. (2000). The Islands of The Bahamas. Montréal: Ulysses Travel Guides.

McNeese, Tim and Goetzmann, William H. (2006)Christopher Columbus and the Discovery of the Americas, Explorers of New Lands. New York: Chelsea House Publishing.

Mills, Carlton (Ed.) (2008). A History of the Turks and Caicos Islands. Oxford: MacMillan Publishers.

Milton, John. (1857). Poetical Works of John Milton. London: George Routledge and Co.

Munroe, Myles. (1992). In Pursuit of Purpose. Pennsylvania: Destiny Images Publishers, Inc.

Pavlac, Brian A. (2011). Concise Survey of Western Civilization: Supremacies and Diversities throughout History-

-Volume II: 1500 to Present. Maryland: Rowman and Littlefield Publishers Inc.

Permenter, Paris and Bigley, John. (2000). The Bahamas: A taste of the Islands. New Jersey: Hunter Publishing, Inc.

Pohl, John and Hook, Adam. (2001). The Conquistador: 1492-1550 (Warrior). Oxford: Osprey Publishing.

Rodriguez, Junius P. (Ed.). (2007). Encyclopedia of Slave Resistance and Rebellion, Volume 1. Connecticut: Greenwood Press.

Room, Adrian (1997).Placenames of the World. California: McFarland and Company, Inc.

Saunders, Gail. (2000). The Bahamas: A Family of Islands. London: Macmillan Education.

Saunders, Nicholas. (Ed.) (2005). The Peoples of the Caribbean: An Encyclopedia of Archaeology and Traditional Culture. California: ABC-CLIO, Inc.

Smith, Jean Reeder and Smith, Baldwin Lacey. (1980). Essentials of World history. New York: Barron's Educational series, Inc.

Spalding, Mark and Bunting, Gillian (2004). A Guide to the Coral Reefs of the Caribbean. California: University of California Press.

Staten, Clifford L. (2005).The History of Cuba.New York, New York: Palgrave Macmillan.

Stausberg, Michael (2011). Religion and Tourism: Crossroads, Destinations and Encounters. New York: Routledge.

Taylor, Alan. (2001). American Colonies: The Settling of North America. New York: Penguin Press.

Taylor, Chris (2012). The Black Carib Wars: Freedom, Survival, and the Making of the Garifuna. Oxford: Signal Books.

The Bahamas Government. (1973). The Bahamas Independence Order. Nassau, Bahamas: Bahamas Government Printing.

The Bahamas Historical Society. (1991). Journal of The Bahamas Historical Society Vol. 13-20. Nassau, Bahamas: The Society.

The Bahamas Historical Society. (2012). The History of The Bahamas in Pictures. Nassau, Bahamas: Media Enterprises Ltd.

Traboulay, David M. (1994) Columbus and Las Casas: The Conquest and Christianization of America, 1492-1566. Maryland: University Press of America, Inc.

Wells, Spencer. (2002). The Journey of Man—A Genetic Odyssey. Princeton University Press: New Jersey.

Woodard, Colin. (2008). The Republic of Pirates: Being the True and Surprising Story of the Caribbean Pirates and the Man Who Brought Them Down. Florida: Harcourt Inc.

Author's Contact

Postal Address:

Tellis Bethel

P.O. Box CB 11990

Nassau, Bahamas

www.BooksByBethel.com

FOOTNOTES

[1] Granberry, Julian and Vescelius, Gary S. (2004). Languages of the Pre-Columbian Antilles. Alabama: The University of Alabama Press, p.80.
[2] The Bahamas Government. (1973). The Bahamas Independence Order. Nassau, Bahamas: Bahamas Government Printing, p. 13.
[3] Parker, Christopher. (2001). Bahamas and Turks and Caicos. (2^{nd}ed.). Victoria, Australia: Lonely Planet Publications, p.28.
[4] Dupuch, Etienne Jr. (2002). Bahamas Handbook 2003. Nassau: Etienne Dupuch Jr. Publications, p.51. Interestingly, Sir Durward Knowles, also a Bahamian, shares the Guinness World Record for the longest span as an Olympic competitor in the category of yachting. Sir Durward's participation in the Olympic spanned 40 years. See: http://www.guinnessworldrecords.com/ records-3000/longest-span-as-an-olympic-competitor-men [Retrieved: 9 June, 2014].
[5] Keegan, William F., Hofman, Corinne L., and Rodriguez, Ramos Reniel. (Ed.) (2013). The Oxford Handbook of Caribbean Archaeology. Oxford: Oxford University Press, p.225.
[6] The Editors of Encyclopædia Britannica. "Melocactus Communis (plant)." Encyclopedia Britannica Online. Encyclopedia Britannica, n.d. [Retrieved: 20 Sep. 2013].
[7] Aceto, Michael and Williams, Jeffrey Payne. Eds. (2003). Contact Englishes of the Eastern Caribbean. Amsterdam: John Benjamin Publishing Company, p.51.
[8] Keegan, William F. and Carlson, Lisabeth A. (2008).Talking Taino: Caribbean Natural History from a Native Perspective. Alabama: University of Alabama Press, p.10.
[9] Spalding, Mark and Bunting, Gillian (2004). A Guide to the Coral Reefs of the Caribbean. California: University of California Press, p.76.
[10] 2010 Census: See: http://statistics.bahamas.gov.bs/download/023796600.pdf [Retrieved: 20 April 2014].
[11] 2010 Census: See: http://www.paho.org/hq/index.php?option=com_docman&task=doc_view&gid=25191&Itemid= [Retrieved: 2010].
[12] Saunders, Nicholas. (Ed.) (2005). The Peoples of the Caribbean: An Encyclopedia of Archaeology and Traditional Culture. ABC-CLIO, Inc. California, p.157.

[13] Craton, Michael and Saunders, Gail. (1992). Islanders in the Stream: A History of the Bahamian People-From Aboriginal times to the end of slavery. Georgia: University of Georgia Press, pp.73-76.
[14] Ibid.
[15] Craton, Michael. (1986). A History of the Bahamas. Ontario, Canada: San Salvador Press, p.61.
[16] Mills, Carlton (Ed.). (2008). A History of the Turks and Caicos Islands. Oxford: MacMillan Publishers, p.2.
[17] Ibid., p.250.
[18] Ibid., pp.132, 250.
[19] Ibid., p.283.
[20] Many people who live in The Bahamas are descendants of the Turks and Caicos Islanders and have made significant contributions toward the development of The Bahamas.
[21] Tinker, Keith. (2011). The Migration of Peoples from the Caribbean to the Bahamas. Florida: University Press of Florida, pp.7-8.
[22] For the purpose of this book, the author treats the peoples of The Bahamas and the Turks and Caicos Islands as one people due to their common geography, history and heritage.
[23] The Bahama chain is also separated from the United States by a fifty-mile-wide marine channel named, the Straits of Florida.
[24] Tinker, Keith. (2012). The African Diaspora to the Bahamas. Victoria, BC, Canada: L. Friesen Press, p.58.
[25] As a part of the Caribbean region, The Bahamas is a member state of the Caribbean Community (CARICOM) consisting of 15 Caribbean States to improve the standards of political, economic and social wellbeing among member states. See: http://www.iccnow.org/?mod=caricom [Retrieved: 27 August 2014]. It is should be noted that before and after The Bahamas achieved independence, many people from around the Caribbean lived, worked and positively contributed to the development of The Bahamas. See: Tinker, Keith. (2012). The African Diaspora to the Bahamas. Victoria, BC, Canada: L. Friesen Press, pp.188-201.
[26] Loven, Sven. (2010). Origins of the Tainan Culture, West Indies. Alabama: University of Alabama Press, p.57.
[27] Keegan, William F. and Carlson, Lisabeth A. (2008). Talking Taino: Caribbean Natural History from a Native Perspective. Alabama: University of Alabama Press, p.11.

[28] Keegan, William F., Hofman, Corinne L. and Rodriguez, Reniel Ramos (Eds.). (2013). The Oxford Handbook of Caribbean Archaeology. Oxford: Oxford University Press, p.11.
[29] Saunders, Nicholas. (Ed.) (2005). The Peoples of the Caribbean: An Encyclopedia of Archaeology and Traditional Culture. California: ABC-CLIO,Inc., p.157.
[30] Castro, Daniel. (2007). Another Face of Empire: Bartolomé de Las Casas, Indigenous Rights, and Ecclesiastical Imperialism. North Carolina: Duke University Press, p.169.
[31] Keegan, William F. and Carlson, Lisabeth A. (2008). Talking Taino: Caribbean Natural History from a Native Perspective. Alabama: University of Alabama Press, p.1.
[32] Curet, Antonio L. and Hauser, Mark W. (Eds.) (2011). Islands at the Crossroads: Migration, Seafaring, and Interaction in the Caribbean. Alabama: The University of Alabama Press, p.132.
[33] Keegan, William F., Hofman, Corinne L., and Rodriguez, Ramos Reniel.(Eds.) (2013). The Oxford Handbook of Caribbean Archaeology. Oxford: Oxford University Press, p.204.
[34] Loven, Sven. (2010). Origins of the Tainan Culture, West Indies. Alabama: University of Alabama Press, p.71.
[35] Ibid., p.1.
[36] Ibid., p.71.
[37] Ibid., p.10.
[38] http://www.bahamapundit.com/2013/07/exploring-the-lucayan-prehistory-of-the-bahamas.html [Retrieved: 21 September, 2013].
[39] Granberry, Julian and Vescelius, Gary S. (2004). Languages of the Pre-Columbian Antilles. Alabama: The University of Alabama Press, pp.80-86.
[40] Barratt, Peter. (2011). Bahama Saga: The epic saga of the Bahama Islands. Indiana: 1stBooks, p.328.
[41] Ibid., pp.327-328.
[42] Allsopp, Richard and Allsopp, Jeannette.(2003). Dictionary of Caribbean English Usage. Kingston, Jamaica: University of the West Indies Press, p.70.
[43] Ibid.
[44] Craton, Michael and Saunders, Gail. (1992). Islanders in the Stream: A History of the Bahamian People-From Aboriginal times to the end of slavery. Georgia: University of Georgia Press, p.5.

[45] Brodsky, David. (2008). Spanish Vocabulary: An Etymological Approach. Texas: University of Texas Press, p.579.
[46] Amy, Jantzer. "LUXURY BAHAMAS RESORT OFFERS FIRST SALES TO CHINESE BUYERS." Release. Baha Mar, 11 May 2012. [Retrieved: 21 December 2013]. As of 2016, the resort filed bankruptcy in Delaware, USA, on 29 June 2014. See: http://www.bloomberg.com/news/articles/2016-01-04/the-ghosts-of-baha-mar-how-a-3-5-billion-paradise-went-bust [Retrieved: 4 September 2016].
[47] https://en.wikipedia.org/wiki/Baha_Mar [Retrieved 21 August 2016].
[48] Marley, David, F. (2005). Historic Cities of the Americas: An Illustrated Encyclopedia, Volume 1: The Caribbean, Mexico, and Central America. Santa Barbara: ABC-CLIO.p.3.
[49] http://www.bahamapundit.com/2013/07/exploring-the-lucayan-prehistory-of-the-bahamas.html [Retrieved: 21 September, 2013].
[50] Granberry, Julian and Vescelius, Gary S. (2004). Languages of the Pre-Columbian Antilles. Alabama: The University of Alabama Press, pp.80-86.
[51] Thompson, G.A. (1812) The Geographical and Historical Dictionary of America and the West Indies, Volume 1. London: Harding and Wright. p.124.
[52] Granberry, Julian and Vescelius, Gary S. (2004). Languages of the Pre-Columbian Antilles. Alabama: The University of Alabama Press, p.80.
[53] Keegan, William F., Hofman, Corinne L., and Rodriguez, Ramos Reniel.(Ed.) (2013). The Oxford Handbook of Caribbean Archaeology. Oxford: Oxford University Press, p.264.
[54] Ibid, p.10.
[55] Ibid, p.71.
[56] Fuson, Robert Henderson. (2000). Juan Ponce de León and the Spanish Discovery of Puerto Rico and Florida. Newark, OH: McDonald & Woodward Publishing Company. pp.88-112.
[57] Eagen Rachel (2006). Ponce de León: Exploring Florida and Puerto Rico. New York: Crabtree Publishing Company. pp. 11-12.
[58] Emmer, Pieter, et al. (1999). General History of the Caribbean. Vol. II: New Societies: The Caribbean in the Long Sixteenth Century. UNESCO Publishing/MacMillan Education Ltd. p.311.
[59] https://www.loc.gov/item/73697197/ [Retrieved 20 august 2016].
[60] https://www.loc.gov/item/74693298/ [Retrieved 20 august 2016].
[61] https://www.loc.gov/item/73697197/ [Retrieved 20 August 2016]

[62] https://en.wikipedia.org/wiki/Placer_(geography) [Retrieved 22 August 2016].
[63] http://maps.bpl.org/id/14999 [retrieved 20 August 2016].
[64] http://hdl.huntington.org/cdm/ref/collection/p15150coll4/id/1490 [retrieved: 20 August 2016].
[65] https://commons.wikimedia.org/wiki/File:1864_Johnson_Map _of_the_West_Indies_and_Caribbean_-_Geographicus_-_WestIndies-johnson-1864.jpg [Retrieved: 20 August 2016].
[66] Rouse, Irving (1992). The Tainos. Yale University Press. pp.21-22; Saunders Nicholas J. (2005). The Peoples of the Caribbean: An Encyclopedia of Archeology and Traditional culture. ABC-CLIO, Inc. California. p.141.
[67] Rouse, Irving (1992). The Tainos. Yale University Press. p.131.
[68]. Ibid. pp.21-22.
[69] Saunders Nicholas J. (2005). The Peoples of the Caribbean: An Encyclopedia of Archeology and Traditional culture. ABC-CLIO, Inc. California, p.141
[70] Rouse, Irving (1992). The Tainos. Yale University Press. pp.21-22.
[71] Saunders Nicholas J. (2005). The Peoples of the Caribbean: An Encyclopedia of Archeology and Traditional culture. ABC-CLIO, Inc. California. p.141.
[72] The dawning of the modern era refers to the beginning of the period known as modern civilization, modern era or modern history (that is, the years immediately before or after 1500 A.D.) See: Smith, Jean Reeder and Smith, Baldwin Lacey. (1980). Essentials of World history. New York: Barron's Educational series, Inc., p.iii. See also: Dunan, Marcel. (1964). Larousse Encyclopedia of Modern History, From 1500 to the Present Day. New York: Harper and Row, 1964.
[73] Keegan, William F., Hofman, Corinne L. and Rodriguez, Reniel Ramos (Eds.). (2013). The Oxford Handbook of Caribbean Archaeology. Oxford: Oxford University Press, p.11.
[74] Ibid.
[75] Ibid.
[76] Keegan, William F. and Carlson, Lisabeth A. (2008).Talking Taino: Caribbean Natural History from a Native Perspective. Alabama: University of Alabama Press, p.2.
[77] Craton, Michael and Saunders, Gail (1999).Islanders in the Stream: A History of the Bahamian People- from aboriginal times to the end of slavery. Georgia: University of Georgia Press, p.29.

[78] Keegan, William F., Hofman, Corinne L. and Rodriguez, Reniel Ramos (Eds.). (2013). The Oxford Handbook of Caribbean Archaeology. Oxford: Oxford University Press, p.11.
[79] Saunders, Nicholas. (Ed.) (2005). The Peoples of the Caribbean: An Encyclopedia of Archaeology and Traditional Culture. California: ABC-CLIO, Inc., p.168.
[80] Craton, Michael and Saunders, Gail. (1992). Islanders in the Stream: A History of the Bahamian People-From Aboriginal times to the end of slavery. Georgia: University of Georgia Press, p.18.
[81] Saunders, Nicholas. (Ed.) (2005). The Peoples of the Caribbean: An Encyclopedia of Archaeology and Traditional Culture. California: ABC-CLIO, Inc., p.168.
[82] Mills, Carlton (Ed.) (2008). A History of the Turks and Caicos Islands. Oxford: MacMillan Publishers, p. 83.
[83] Craton, Michael and Saunders, Gail (1999) Islanders in the Stream: A History of the Bahamian People- from aboriginal times to the end of slavery. Georgia: University of Georgia Press, pp.8-9.
[84] Higman, B. W. (2011) A Concise History of the Caribbean. New York: Cambridge University Press, pp.10-12.
[85] Ibid.
[86] Moure, Ramon Dacal and Rivero, Manuel de La Calle. (1996). Art and Archaeology of Pre-Columbian Cuba. Pennsylvania: University of Pittsburgh Press, pp.22-24.
[87] Ibid.
[88] Ibid.
[89] Keegan, William F., Hofman, Corinne L. and Rodriguez, Reniel Ramos (Eds.). (2013). The Oxford Handbook of Caribbean Archaeology. Oxford: Oxford University Press, p.11.
[90] Keegan, William F. and Carlson, Lisabeth A. (2008) Talking Taino: Caribbean Natural History from a Native Perspective. Alabama: University of Alabama Press, p.1.
[91] Boucher, Philip P. (1992). Cannibal Encounters: Europeans and Island Caribs,1492–1763. Maryland: John Hopkins University, p.1632.
[92] Keegan, William F. and Carlson, Lisabeth A. (2008) Talking Taino: Caribbean Natural History from a Native Perspective. Alabama: University of Alabama Press, p.10.
[93] Taylor, Chris (2012). The Black Carib Wars: Freedom, Survival, and the Making of the Garifuna. Oxford: Signal Books, p.6.

[94] Courtz, Henk (2008). A Carib Grammar and Dictionary. Toronto: Magoria Books, p.1.
[95] Taylor, Chris (2012). The Black Carib Wars: Freedom, Survival, and the Making of the Garifuna. Oxford: Signal Books, p.4.
[96] Boucher, Philip P. (1992). Cannibal Encounters: Europeans and Island Caribs, 1492–1763. Maryland: John Hopkins University, p.1632.
[97] Ibid.
[98] Loven, Sven. (2010). Origins of the Tainan Culture, West Indies. Alabama: University of Alabama Press, pp.57-58.
[99] Boucher, Philip P. (1992). Cannibal Encounters: Europeans and Island Caribs, 1492–1763. Maryland: John Hopkins University Press, p.1632.
[100] Saunders, Nicholas. (Ed.) (2005). The Peoples of the Caribbean: An Encyclopedia of Archaeology and Traditional Culture. ABC-CLIO, Inc. California, p.45.
[101] Melion, Walter S., Rothstein Bret, Weemans Michel. (eds.) (2015). The Anthropomorphic Lens: Anthropomorphism, Microcosm and Analogy in Early Modern Thought and Visual Arts. Boston: Brill.p.98.
[102] Ibid.
[103] Arens, William. (1979). The Man-Eating Myth: Anthropology and Anthropophagy. London: Oxford University Press, p.44.
[104] Boucher, Philip P. (1992). Cannibal Encounters: Europeans and Island Caribs, 1492–1763. Maryland: John Hopkins University Press, pp.1632, 1633, 1636 and 1638.
[105] Ibid., p.1633.
[106] Ibid., pp.1632, 1633, 1636 and 1638.
[107] Palmié, Stephan and Scarano, Francisco A. (Eds.) (2011).The Caribbean: A History of the Region and Its Peoples. Chicago: University of Chicago Press, p.27.
[108] http://dominicanewsonline.com/news/homepage/news/general/change-from-carib-to-kalinago-now-official/ {Retrieved: 4 September 2016].
[109] Saunders, Nicholas. (Ed.) (2005). The Peoples of the Caribbean: An Encyclopedia of Archaeology and Traditional Culture. California: ABC-CLIO, Inc., p.149.
[110] Ibid., p.161.
[111] Courtz, Henk (2008). A Carib Grammar and Dictionary. Toronto: Magoria Books, p.3.
[112] Ibid., p.1.

[113] The Arawaks and Caribs had inhabited the Virgin Islands. The Caribs were apparently raiding the east coast of Puerto Rico at the time of Columbus. See: Dookhan, Isaac. (1994) A History of the Virgin Islands of the United States. P.16
[114] Cobley, Alan (1994) Crossroads of Empire: The Europe-Caribbean Connection 1492-1992. Cave Hill, Barbados: The Department of History, University of the West Indies, pp. 24-28.
[115] Cited in: Craton, Michael. (1986) A History of the Bahamas. San Salvador Press. p.21.
[116] Craton, Michael. (1986) A History of the Bahamas. San Salvador Press. p.11.
[117] Ibid p.21.
[118] Ibid. pp.19-20. Keegan, William F. (1992). The People Who Discovered Columbus: The Prehistory of the Bahamas. University Press of Florida. p.183.
[119] Albury, Paul. (1975) The Story of the Bahamas. MacMillan Caribbean. pp.17-18. Craton, Michael. (1986). A History of the Bahamas. San Salvador Press. p.17.
[120] Craton, Michael. (1986) A History of the Bahamas. San Salvador Press. p.24.
[121] Conrad, Geoffrey W., John W. Foster, and Charles D. Beeker, "Organic artifacts from the Manantial de la Aleta, Dominican Republic: preliminary observations and interpretations",Journal of Caribbean Archaeology. 2:6, 2001. Albury, Paul. (1975) The Story of the Bahamas. MacMillan Caribbean. pp.17-18. Craton, Michael. (1986) A History of the Bahamas. San Salvador Press. p.17.
[122] Craton, Michael and Saunders, Gail. (1992). Islanders in the Stream: A History of the Bahamian People-From Aboriginal times to the end of slavery. Georgia: University of Georgia Press, p.47.
[123] Craton, Michael. (1986) A History of the Bahamas. San Salvador Press. pp.24, 26.
[124] Ibid. p.18.
[125] Albury, Paul. (1975) The Story of the Bahamas. MacMillan Caribbean. pp.14-16. Craton, Michael. (1986) A History of the Bahamas. San Salvador Press. pp. 17, 18, 17, 20-21. Sauer, Carl Ortwin. (1966; Fourth printing, 1992) The Early Spanish Main. University of California Press. pp.30-31.

[126] Craton, Michael and Saunders, Gail. (1992). Islanders in the Stream: A History of the Bahamian People-From Aboriginal times to the end of slavery. Georgia: University of Georgia Press, p.39.
[127] Flores, Lisa Pierce. (2010). The History of Puerto Rico. Santa Barbara: Greenwood Press.p.18.
[128] Craton, Michael and Saunders, Gail. (1992). Islanders in the Stream: A History of the Bahamian People-From Aboriginal times to the end of slavery. Georgia: University of Georgia Press, p.39.
[129] Albury, Paul. (1975) The Story of the Bahamas. MacMillan Caribbean. pp.17-18. Craton, Michael. (1986) A History of the Bahamas. San Salvador Press. p.13.
[130] Craton, Michael. (1986) A History of the Bahamas. San Salvador Press. p.21.
[131] Ibid. p.20.
[132] Albury, Paul. (1975) The Story of the Bahamas. MacMillan Caribbean. pp.17-18. Craton, Michael. (1986) A History of the Bahamas. San Salvador Press. pp 14-16.
[133] Craton, Michael. (1986) A History of the Bahamas. San Salvador Press. pp.20, 24.
[134] Ibid. pp.14-20.
[135] Ibid. p.23.
[136] Saunders, Nicholas. (Ed.) (2005). The Peoples of the Caribbean: An Encyclopedia of Archaeology and Traditional Culture. ABC-CLIO, Inc. California, pp.169, 405.
[137] Keegan, William F. (1992). The People Who Discovered Columbus: The Prehistory of the Bahamas. University Press of Florida. pp.124-127. Craton, Michael. (1986) A History of the Bahamas. San Salvador Press. pp.20, 25.
[138] Albury, Paul. (1975) The Story of the Bahamas. MacMillan Caribbean. pp.17-18. Craton, Michael. (1986) A History of the Bahamas. San Salvador Press. pp.20, 24-25. Granberry, Julian & Gary S. Vescelius. (2004) Languages of the Pre-Columbian Antilles. The University of Alabama Press. p.43. Keegan, William F. (1992). The People Who Discovered Columbus: The Prehistory of the Bahamas. University Press of Florida. pp.52-53,77.
[139] Craton, Michael. (1986) A History of the Bahamas. San Salvador Press. pp.19-20, 24.
[140] Keegan, William F. (1992) The People Who Discovered Columbus: The Prehistory of the Bahamas. University Press of Florida. pp.166-167

Sauer, Carl Ortwin. (1966; Fourth printing, 1992) The Early Spanish Main. University of California Press. p.62. Albury, Paul. (1975) The Story of the Bahamas. MacMillan Caribbean. pp.17-18. Craton, Michael. (1986) A History of the Bahamas. San Salvador Press. p.23.
[141] Craton, Michael. (1986) A History of the Bahamas. San Salvador Press. p.24.
[142] Ibid. p.21.
[143] Ibid. p.23.
[144] Ibid. p.18. By 1985, over 175 sites were identified.
[145] http://etymonline.com/ [Retrieved: 21 Jan. 2014].
[146] Ibid.
[147] Cleare, Angela, B. (2007). History of Tourism in The Bahamas: A Global Perspective. Indiana: Xlibris Corp, pp.25-26.
[148] Funk, Wilfred. (1998). Word Origins: An Exploration and History of Words and Language. New York: Wings Books, p.331.
[149] See: https://genographic.nationalgeographic.com/human-journey/ [Retrieved: 30 Aug. 2013].
[150] Wells, Spencer. (2002). The Journey of Man—A Genetic Odyssey. Princeton University Press: New Jersey, p.138.
[151] "Native American Populations Descend from Three Key Migrations, Scientists Say." ScienceDaily." ScienceDaily, 11 July 2012. [Retrieved: 12 Oct. 2013].
[152] Wells, Spencer. (2002). The Journey of Man—A Genetic Odyssey. Princeton University Press: New Jersey, p.141.
[153] Craton, Michael and Saunders, Gail (1999) Islanders in the Stream: A History of the Bahamian People- from aboriginal times to the end of slavery. Georgia: University of Georgia Press, p.9.
[154] Moure, Ramon Dacal and Rivero, Manuel de La Calle. (1996). Art and Archaeology of Pre-Columbian Cuba. Pennsylvania: University of Pittsburgh Press, p.15.
[155] Wells, Spencer. (2002). The Journey of Man—A Genetic Odyssey. New Jersey: Princeton University Press, p.138, p.142.
[156] Bradley, Bruce and Stanford, Dennis. (2004). The North Atlantic ice-edge corridor: a possible Palaeolithic route to the New World. World Archaeology. 36(4): 459-478.
[157] Stausberg, Michael (2011). Religion and Tourism: Crossroads, Destinations and Encounters. New York: Routledge, p.128.
[158] See: http://www.atlantisbahamas.com/thingstodo/marinehabitat [Retrieved: 20 Dec. 2013].

[159] McNeese, Tim and Goetzmann, William H. (2006). Christopher Columbus and the Discovery of the Americas, Explorers of New Lands. New York: Chelsea House Publishing, p.50.
[160] Kohen, Elizabeth, Elias and Marie Louise.(2013). Spain. New York: Marshall Cavendish Benchmark, pp.19-21.
[161] Smith, Jean Reeder and Smith, Lacey Baldwin (1980). Essentials of World history. London: Barron Educational Series, pp.76-77.
[162] Pletcher, Kenneth. (Ed.) (2010). The Britannica Guide to Explorers and Explorations That Changed the Modern World. New York: Educational Publishing Britannica Educational Publishing, pp.60-61.
[163] San Salvador Island is home to the Cyclura rileyi, which is also called the San Salvador Iguana and is an endangered species of lizard in the genus Cyclura in The Bahamas. See: http://www.arkive.org/san-salvador-iguana/cyclura-rileyi [Retrieved: 27 August 2014].
[164] Craton, Michael and Saunders, Gail. (1999).Islanders in the Stream: A History of the Bahamian People- from aboriginal times to the end of slavery. Georgia. University of Georgia Press, p.21.
[165] Ibid., p.48.
[166] Ibid., p.49.
[167] Granberry, Julian and Vescelius, Gary S. (2004). Languages of the Pre-Columbian Antilles. Alabama: The University of Alabama Press, p.85.
[168] Cadigan, Sean Thomas (2009). Newfoundland and Labrador: A History. Toronto: University of Toronto Press Inc., pp.27-28.
[169] Kolesnikov-Jessop, Sonia. "Did Chinese Beat out Columbus?" Arts. New York Times, 25 June 2005. [Retrieved: 24 Sept. 2013].
[170] Menzies, Gavin. (2004). 1421: The Year China Discovered America. New York: HarperCollins Publishers Inc., p. 303.
[171] Belling, Larry (Actor) and Wallace, David (Director) (2004). 1421: The Year China Discovered America? PBS: Documentary. See: Andrea, Alfred and Overfield, James. (2011). The Human Record: Sources of Global History, Volume I: To 1500. Boston: Cengage Learning, p.408.
[172] Joseph, Frank and Sitchin, Zecharia. (Eds.). (2006). Discovering the Mysteries of Ancient America: Lost History and Legends Unearthed and Explored. Career Press, Inc., pp. 210-217.
[173] More specifically, just about all of the modern nations, overseas territories, and their peoples that exist within the Americas today, and the sequence of events that followed came about as a result of Christopher Columbus' first landfall in the Lucayan chain in the Americas. It should be noted, however, that for the purpose of this

book, the term modern nations refers to those European colonies within the Americas that had evolved since the time of Columbus to become sovereign states under the United Nations. See: http://www.un.org/en/members [Retrieved: 27 August 2014]. It should also be noted that there are Native Americans in Canada today, who refer to themselves as First Nation, but their Reserves are not recognized as independent states. [See: http://www.aadnc-aandc.gc.ca/eng/1100100014642/1100100014643. Retrieved: 27 August 2014]. Nevertheless, their heritage and lineage within the modern Americas originated centuries (or even millennia) before the arrival of Columbus in the Americas. Many of these persons, as well as their descendants, were adversely impacted as a result of the events that followed Columbus' landfall in the Americas.

[174] Masur, Louis P. (ed.) (1999). The Challenge of American History. Maryland: John Hopkins University Press, p.31.

[175] Markham, Clements R. (Ed.). (2010).Letters of Amerigo Vespucci, and Other Documents Illustrative of His Career. New York: Cambridge University Press, p.xviii.

[176] Craton, Michael and Saunders, Gail (1999) Islanders in the Stream: A History of the Bahamian People-from aboriginal times to the end of slavery. Georgia: University of Georgia Press, pp.405.

[177] Ibid., pp.405.

[178] The 17th century British pirate, George Watling, after whom the island was named, is said to have claimed the island for himself. See: Parker, Christopher. (2001). Bahamas and Turks and Caicos. (2nded.). Victoria, Australia: Lonely Planet Publications, p.373.

[179] Dupuch, Etienne Jr. (2003) Bahamas Handbook. Nassau: Etienne Dupuch Jr. Publications, pp.67, 72.

[180] http://www.geraceresearchcentre.com/pdfs/1stColumbus/173_FusonRH_1stColumbus.pdf [Retrieved: 3 September 2016]

[181] McKinnen, Daniel. (1804). A Tour Through the British West Indies, in the Years 1802 and 1803, Giving a Particular Account of The Bahama Islands. London: Taylor Black-Horse Court, pp. 198-201.

[182] Each year, hundreds of cruise ship passengers visit Half Moon Cay at Little San Salvador for relaxation and recreation.

[183] Dupuch, Etienne Jr. (2003) Bahamas Handbook. Nassau: Etienne Dupuch Jr. Publications, p.68.

[184] Dupuch, Etienne, Jr. (1992). Bahamas Handbook and Businessman's Annual. Nassau: E. Dupuch, Jr., Publications, p. 31.
[185] Gerace, Donald T. "Publications" "The First San Salvador conference; Columbus and his World. Gerace Research Centre, 1987. [Retrieved: 19 Apr. 2014].
[186] Saunders, Nicholas. (Ed.) (2005). The Peoples of the Caribbean: An Encyclopedia of Archaeology and Traditional Culture. ABC-CLIO, Inc. California, pp.169, 405.
[187] Dupuch, Etienne Jr. (2003) Bahamas Handbook. Nassau: Etienne Dupuch Jr. Publications, p.65.
[188] http://www.geraceresearchcentre.com/pdfs/1stColumbus/173_FusonRH_1stColumbus.pdf [Retrieved: 3 September 2016]
[189] Barratt, Peter. (2011). Bahama Saga: The Epic Story of the Bahama Islands. Indiana: 1stBooks, p.328.
[190] Dupuch, Etienne Jr. (2003) Bahamas Handbook. Nassau: Etienne Dupuch Jr. Publications, p.66.
[191] Curet, Antonio L. and Hauser, Mark W. (Ed.) (2011). Islands at the Crossroads: Migration, Seafaring, and Interaction in the Caribbean. Alabama: The University of Alabama Press, p.110.
[192] Ibid., p.112.
[193] Fernández-Armesto, Felipe.(2008). Columbus on Himself. Indiana: Hackett Publishing, Inc., pp.69, 70.
[194] Bodmer, Beatriz Pastor (1992). The Armature of Conquest: Spanish Accounts of the Discovery of America, 1492 – 1589. California: Stanford University Press, p.24.
[195] Senauth, Frank. (2011). The Making and the Destruction of Haiti. Indiana: Author House, p.1.
[196] "Hispañiola." Genocide Studies Program. Yale University, 2010. [Retrieved: 24 Sep. 2013].
[197] Saunders, Nicholas. (Ed.) (2005). The Peoples of the Caribbean: An Encyclopedia of Archaeology and Traditional Culture. ABC-CLIO, Inc. California, p.157.
[198] Maclean, Frances. "Lost Fort of Columbus." Smithsonian.com. Smithsonian Magazine, Jan. 2008. [Retrieved: 24 Sep. 2013].
[199] Senauth, Frank. (2011). The Making and the Destruction of Haiti. Indiana: Author House, p.1.

[200] The British Crown had granted the Bahama Islands to Attorney General, Sir Robert Heath. Craton, Michael. (1986). A History of the Bahamas. Ontario, Canada: San Salvador Press, p.50.
[201] Craton, Michael and Saunders, Gail. (1999). Islanders in the Stream: A History of the Bahamian People: Volume One: From Aboriginal Times to the End of Slavery. Athens, Georgia: The university of Georgia Press, pp.74-78.
[202] Encyclopaedia Britannica. "The Fourth and Final Years." Encyclopaedia Britannica, n.d., [Retrieved: 19 April, 2014].
[203] Masur, Louis P. (Ed.) (1999). The Challenge of American History. Maryland: John Hopkins University Press, p.28.
[204] Markham, Clements R. (Ed.). (2010).Letters of Amerigo Vespucci, and Other Documents Illustrative of His Career. New York: Cambridge University Press, p.xviii.
[205] Room, Adrian (1997). Placenames of the World. California: McFarland and Company, Inc., p.28.
[206] Milton, John. (1857). Poetical Works of John Milton. London: George Routledge and Co., p.330.
[207] See: https://www.britannica.com/biography/Christopher-Columbus/The-fourth-voyage-and-final-years [Retrieved: 19 April, 2014].
[208] Rodriguez, Junius P. (Ed.). (2007). Encyclopedia of Slave Resistance and Rebellion, Volume 1. Connecticut: Greenwood Press, pp.227-228.
[209] Craton, Michael and Saunders, Gail (1999) Islanders in the Stream: A History of the Bahamian People: Volume One: From Aboriginal Times to the End of Slavery. Georgia: University of Georgia Press, p.53.
[210] Keegan, William F. and Carlson, Lisabeth A. (2008) Talking Taino: Caribbean Natural History from a Native Perspective. Alabama: University of Alabama Press, p.7.
[211] Vickery, Paul S. (2006). Bartolomé de Las Casas: Great Prophet of the Americas. Volume 13, New Jersey: Paulist Press, p.54.
[212] Craton, Michael and Saunders, Gail. (1999). Islanders in the Stream: A History of the Bahamian People: Volume One: From Aboriginal Times to the End of Slavery. Athens, Georgia: The University of Georgia Press, p.43.
[213] Vickery, Paul S. (2006). Bartolomé de Las Casas: Great Prophet of the Americas. Volume 13, New Jersey: Paulist Press, p.54.

[214] The Lucayans and Tainos were classic animists, who worshipped spirits of the sun, moon, trees and other natural objects. Brown, Isabel Zakrzewski. (1999). Culture and Customs of the Dominican Republic. Connecticut: Greenwood Press, p.73.
[215] Figueredo, D. H. and Argote-Freyre, Frank. (2008). A Brief History of the Caribbean. New York: Facts on File, Inc., pp.21-22.
[216] Loven, Sven. (2010). Origins of the Tainan Culture, West Indies. Alabama: University of Alabama Press, p.69.
[217] Ferguson, Moira (1994). Jamaica Kincaid: Where the Land Meets the Body. Virginia: University Press of Virginia, p.139.
[218] Saunders, Nicholas. (Ed.) (2005). The Peoples of the Caribbean: An Encyclopedia of Archaeology and Traditional Culture. ABC-CLIO, Inc. California, p.169.
[219] Keegan, William F., Hofman, Corinne L., and Rodriguez, Ramos Reniel. (Eds.) (2013). The Oxford Handbook of Caribbean Archaeology. Oxford: Oxford University Press, p.275.
[220] Keegan, William F. and Carlson, Lisabeth A. (2008) Talking Taino: Caribbean Natural History from a Native Perspective. Alabama: University of Alabama Press, p.8.
[221] Craton, Michael and Saunders, Gail (1999) Islanders in the Stream: A History of the Bahamian People-from aboriginal times to the end of slavery. Georgia: University of Georgia Press, p.26.
[222] Ibid.
[223] Keegan, William F., Hofman, Corinne L., and Rodriguez, Ramos Reniel. (Eds.) (2013). The Oxford Handbook of Caribbean Archaeology. Oxford: Oxford University Press, p.275.
[224] Ibid.
[225] Keegan, William F. and Carlson, Lisabeth A. (2008) Talking Taino: Caribbean Natural History from a Native Perspective. Alabama: University of Alabama Press, p.8.
[226] Ibid.
[227] The Bahamas Historical Society. (1991). Journal of the Bahamas Historical Society Vol. 13-20. Nassau, Bahamas: The Society, p.24.
[228] Craton, Michael and Saunders, Gail (1999) Islanders in the Stream: A History of the Bahamian People- from aboriginal times to the end of slavery. Georgia: University of Georgia Press, pp.74-91.
[229] Pavlac, Brian A. (2011). Concise Survey of Western Civilization: Supremacies and Diversities throughout History--Volume II: 1500 to Present. Maryland: Rowman and Littlefield Publishers Inc., p.195.

[230] Tinker, Keith (2012). The African Diaspora to the Bahamas. Victoria, BC, Canada: L. Friesen Press. pp.55-58.
[231] Tinker, Keith (2012). The African Diaspora to the Bahamas. Victoria, BC, Canada: L. Friesen Press. pp.55-58.
[232] Klein, Herbert S. (2010). The Atlantic Slave Trade. New York: Cambridge University Press, pp. 193-196.
[233] Howard, Rosalyn. The "Wild Indians" of Andros Island: Black Seminole Legacy in the Bahamas. Journal of Black Studies. Vol. 37, No.2 (Nov., 2006). Sage Publications, Inc. pp275-298.
[234] Ibid.
[235] Ibid.
[236] Ibid.
[237] Pencak, William. (2011) Historical Dictionary of Colonial America. Maryland: Scarecrow Press, Inc., p.xiv.
[238] Pohl, John and Hook, Adam. (2001). The Conquistador: 1492-1550 (Warrior). Oxford: Osprey Publishing, p.12.
[239] Bernstein, Peter L. (2012). The Power of Gold: The History of an Obsession. New Jersey: John Wiley & Sons, Inc., p.135.
[240] http://www.historymuseum.ca/cmc/exhibitions/civil/maya/mmc09eng.shtml {Retrieved: 4 September 2016}.
[241] Senauth, Frank. (2011). The Making and the Destruction of Haiti. Indiana: Author House, pp.1-3.
[242] Findling, John E. and Thackeray, Frank W. (2000). Events that changed America through the Seventeenth Century. London: Greenwood Press. p.21.
[243] Worldatlas. "Caribbean TIMELINE." Caribbean Timeline. World Atlas, n.d. [Retrieved: 23 Sept. 2013].
[244] Woodard, Colin. (2008). The Republic of Pirates: Being the True and Surprising Story of the Caribbean Pirates and the Man Who Brought Them Down. Florida: Harcourt Inc., p.2.
[245] Konstam, Angus. (1998). Pirates: 1660–1730. Oxford: Osprey Publishing. pp. 1-7.
[246] Craton, Michael and Saunders, Gail. (1999). Islanders in the Stream: A History of the Bahamian People: Volume One: From Aboriginal Times to the End of Slavery. Athens, Georgia: The university of Georgia Press, pp.pp113-116.
[247] Ibid.

[248] Findling, John E. and Thackeray, Frank W. (2000). Events that changed America through the Seventeenth Century. London: Greenwood Press. p.21.
[249] Forte, Maximilian Christian. (2006).Indigenous Resurgence in the Contemporary Caribbean: Amerindian Survival And Revival. New York: Peter Lang Publishing, Inc., pp.60-64.
[250] Brown, Keith and Olgilvie, Sarah. (2009). Concise Encyclopedia of Languages of the World. Oxford: Elsevier Ltd., p.59.
[251] Saunders, Nicholas. (Ed.) (2005). The Peoples of the Caribbean: An Encyclopedia of Archaeology and Traditional Culture. California: ABC-CLIO, Inc.
[252] Ibid., p.161.
[253] Taylor, Chris (2012). The Black Carib Wars: Freedom, Survival, and the Making of the Garifuna. Oxford: Signal Books, p.4.
[254] The Bahamas Historical Society. (1991). Journal of the Bahamas Historical Society Vol. 13-20. Nassau, Bahamas: The Society, p.24.
[255] Craton, Michael and Saunders, Gail (1999) Islanders in the Stream: A History of the Bahamian People- from aboriginal times to the end of slavery. Georgia: University of Georgia Press, p.58.
[256] Sandler, Michael. (2011). Bridges: Catastrophic Storms. New York: Benchmark Education Company, LLC. p.4.
[257] Saunders, Nicholas. (Ed.) (2005). The Peoples of the Caribbean: An Encyclopedia of Archaeology and Traditional Culture. ABC-CLIO, Inc. California, p.160.
[258] Keegan, William F., Hofman, Corinne L., and Rodriguez, Ramos Reniel.(Ed.) (2013). The Oxford Handbook of Caribbean Archaeology. Oxford: Oxford University Press.p.268.
[259] Granberry, Julian. "Lucayan Toponyms."BAHAMAS HISTORICAL SOCIETY. Journal of the Bahamas Historical Society, Volume 13 (October 1991), n.d. [Retrieved: 1 Sep. 2013].
[260] Keegan, William F. and Carlson, Lisabeth A. (2008).Talking Taino: Caribbean Natural History from a Native Perspective. Alabama: University of Alabama Press, p.10.
[261] Spalding, Mark and Bunting, Gillian (2004). A Guide to the Coral Reefs of the Caribbean. California: University of California Press, p.76.
[262] Jain, Jitendra. (2007). Tracing the Origin and Exploring the Causes and Consequences of Globalization. Norderstedt, Germany: Druck und Bindung—Books on Demand, GmbH, p.5. Columbus took several of the Lucayans as guides aboard his ship prior to leaving The Bahamas. See:

Craton, Michael. (1986). A History of The Bahamas. Ontario, Canada: San Salvador Press, p.35.

[263] While it does not justify European oppression of the Amerindians during the post-Columbian era, it should be noted that many European-type atrocities were also committed by indigenous Native Americans against other Native Americans before the arrival of Europeans in the New World. Even the Caribs were known to attack Arawakan tribes killing the men and enslaving their women. See: Richardson, Bonham C. (1992). The Caribbean in the Wider World, 1492-1992: A Regional Geography. Cambridge: The Press Syndicate of the University of Cambridge, p.22.

[264] The Bahamas Government. (1973). The Bahamas Independence Order. Nassau, Bahamas: Bahamas Government Printing, p. 13.

[265] The United Nations Declaration of Human Rights was produced in 1948 for the preservation of humanity. http://www.un.org/en/universal-declaration-human-rights/ .[Retrieved: 3 September 2016]. The Declaration came on the heels of World War II (1939 – 1945), which saw 60 million casualties, much of it caused by Adolph Hitler's (the then Chancellor of Germany) quest for global dominion, the wealth of the nations, and the pleasure this would have brought at the expense of the weak or helpless.

[266] Kelly, Scott [ScottKelly@StationCDRKelly]. (2016, 8 August) I knew it! The waters in the #Bahamas are as beautiful on Earth as they are from space! https://t.co/uGkm5e18yK [Tweet]. Retrieved from (https://twitter.com/StationCDRKelly/status/762791398164664320?s=02)

[267]The Bahamas Government. (1973). The Bahamas Independence Order. Nassau, Bahamas: Bahamas Government Printing, p. 13.

[268] The predominant view of many scholars and researchers suggest that the first settlers in the Americas came by way of Beringia (that is, the land bridge that once existed between eastern Russia (in Asia) and Alaska (in North America), which means that the unfolding of the ancient Americas would have originated from Alaska, which would have made Alaska the birthplace of the ancient Americas.

[269] The name 'Lucayan Sea' would encompass that area of water currently consisting of The Bahamas' and the Turks and Caicos Islands' territorial seas, as well as their contiguous and exclusive economic zones as provided for by the United Nations Convention on the Law of

the Sea (1982). Both The Bahamas and the Turks and Caicos Islands are party to this convention. See:
United Nations Convention on the Law of the Sea (1982): United Nations. "Overview - Convention & Related Agreements." United Nations Convention on the Law of the Sea of 10 December 1982 Overview and Full Text. UN Oceans and Law of the Sea, A Division for Ocean Affairs and the Law of the Sea, 22 Aug. 2013. [Retrieved: 19 Sep. 2013].

[270] A 'sea' is generally defined as a 'part of the ocean partially enclosed by land.' See: http://oceanservice.noaa.gov/facts/oceanorsea.html [Retrieved 4 September 2016]. Note: The Sargasso Sea, located entirely within the Atlantic Ocean, is the only sea without a land boundary. See: http://oceanservice.noaa.gov/facts/sargassosea.html [Retrieved 4 September 2016].

[271] See: The United Nations Convention on the Law of the Sea. http://www.un.org/depts/los/convention_agreements/texts/unclos/unclos_e.pdf. [Retrieved: 4 Sept. 2016].

[272] McMorran, Jennifer. (2000). The Islands of The Bahamas, Montréal: Ulysses Travel Guides, p. 75.

[273] http://www.spacestory.com/bahamas.htm [Retrieved: 25 September 2013].

[274] UNESCO is an organization of the United Nations that promotes the preservation and protection of natural and cultural heritage at national and international levels. See: United Nations. "States Parties: Ratification Status. "States Parties." United Nations Educational, Scientific and Cultural Organization, 19 Sept. 2012. [Retrieved: 7 Sep. 2013]. The criteria for nomination as a UNESCO World Heritage Site is found at: http://whc.unesco.org/en/nominations/ [Retrieved: 7 Sep. 2013].

[275] The original name for the Gulf of Mexico was Golfo de la Nueva España as recorded on the 1544 map published by Sebastian Cabot. It was later named Golfo Mexicano on the Zaltieri map (1566?). 'All such early inclusive names were given by cartographers and compilers in Europe, and were not derived from local usage, and were not used by those who sailed on such waters.' See: Sauer, Carl Ortwin (1966). The Early Spanish Main. Los Angeles: University of California Press. pp.1-2.

[276] Ibid.

[277] Ibid.

[278] https://en.wikipedia.org/wiki/Pacific_Ocean

[279] http://blog.oxforddictionaries.com/2015/06/water-water-everywhere-ocean-names/
[280] Sauer, Carl Ortwin (1966) The Early Spanish Main. Los Angeles: University of California Press. pp.1-2.
[281] Ibid.
[282] Ibid.
[283] This struggle, however, is not only unique to the people of these islands. Efforts to define the Canadian identity, for example, have been described as "elusive as the Sasquatch and Ogopogo. It has animated—and frustrated—generations of statesmen, historians, writers, artists, philosophers, and the National Film Board... Canada resists easy definition." See: Cohen, Andrew. (2007). The Unfinished Canadian: The People We Are. Toronto: McClelland & Stewart, p. 3.
[284] 1973 was the year The Bahamas obtained its independence from Great Britain, and for the first time the British Government appointed a Governor (Alexander Graham Mitchell) for the Turks and Caicos Islands. Prior to this, the Turks and Caicos Islands was administered on separate occasions by governors of The Bahamas and Jamaica. See: http://www.worldstatesmen.org/Turks_Caicos.html [Retrieved: 4 September 2016].
[285] Johnson, Doris, L. (1972). The Quiet Revolution in The Bahamas. Nassau, Bahamas: Family Islands Press, p.178.
[286] See: http://www.washingtontimes.com/news/2008/jun/08/americas-identity-crisis [Retrieved: 21 August 2014]. The Bradley Project was established by the Lynde and Harry Bradley Foundation
[287] Clodfelter, Michael. (2001). Warfare and Armed Conflicts – A Statistical Reference to Casualty and Other Figures, 1500–2000 (2nd ed.). Jefferson, N.C.: McFarland. pp.584-591.
[288] Burke Peter. (2008). What is Cultural History? Cambridge: Polity, pp.28-29.
[289] Throughout 2014, The Bahamas Ministry of Tourism will be celebrating 50 years since the 'Promotion of Tourism Act' was passed in Parliament in 1964 giving way to the establishment of the country's modern Ministry of Tourism. See: "2014 Declared the 'Year of Culture'" The Tribune 242. N.p., 6 Jan. 2014. [Retrieved: 21 Jan. 2014].
[290] The people of The Bahamas and Turks and Caicos Islands are traditionally a 'friendly' people. See: Saunders, Gail. (2000). The Bahamas: A Family of Islands. Oxford: Macmillan Education, Ltd., p.8.

See also: Jayawardena, Chandana. (2002). Tourism and Hospitality Education and Training in the Caribbean. Jamaica: University of West Indies Press, p.250.

[291] Over the years, many leaders from near and afar have enjoyed the peaceful ambience of these islands. Among them were British Prime Minister, Sir Winston Churchill, United States President, John F. Kennedy, and theologian and black civil rights leader, Reverend, Dr., Martin Luther King Jr. In 1964, Dr. King wrote, in part, his Nobel Peace Prize acceptance speech in Bimini Island in the northern Bahamas. See: Kotz, Nick. (2005). Judgment Days: Lyndon Baines Johnson, Rev. Dr. Martin LutherKing, Jr., and the Laws that changed America. New York: Mariner Books, p.230. Dr. King's famous 'I've been to the Mountain Top' speech was also said to have been written in Bimini in 1968. A few days later, the civil-rights leader was assassinated a day after he delivered his speech to sanitation workers in Memphis, Tennessee. Today, a bronze bust of Dr. King is mounted in Alice Town, Bimini, which is fifty miles west of Miami, Florida, in memory of his visits to that island in 1964 and in 1968. See: http://www.tourismtoday.com/news/bahamas-pays-tribute-dr-martin-luther-king-jr [Retrieved:4 September 2016].

[292] Merriam-Webster Dictionary defines 'purpose' as, 'the reason why something is done or used.' See: www.merriam-webster.com [Retrieved: 21 September 2013]. The purpose of an individual or nation is closely related to that individual's or nation's identity. 'Identity' defines 'who you are' due to a belief or commitment. 'Purpose,' however, defines 'why you do what you do' because of who you are. Hence, a commitment to peace (identity) would involve solving specific problems/meeting of needs related to peace (purpose) in a unique way (culture).

[293] Ambassadors of peace include individuals, groups or business entities (governmental, non-governmental or private) that commit themselves to fostering or promoting the values of peace that are indigenous or natural to the inhabitants of these islands (such as personal health, environmental integrity, and caring for each other).

[294] See: Bahamas Blows Away Guinness World Record for Independence Day: www.guinnessworldrecords.com [Retrieved: 4 September 2016].

[295] http://www.bahamas.com/resources/nassau-accord-1985 [Retrieved: 4 September 2016].

[296] See: Taneka Thompson. "Nelson Mandela dies at 95." Nassau Guardian [Retrieved: 13 Dec. 2013].

[297] Dupuch, Etienne Jr. (2003) Bahamas Handbook. Nassau: Etienne Dupuch Jr. Publications, p.72.
[298] See: Smith, Dana. "National Heroes Day Formally Established." Tribune 242. The Tribune, 11 Oct. 2013. [Retrieved: 21 Dec. 2013].
[299] Miller, Debra and Gonner, Corry. (2005) Caribbean Islands. California: Lonely Planet Books. p. 118.
[300] See: Kotz, Nick. (2005). Judgment Days: Lyndon Baines Johnson, Rev. Dr. Martin LutherKing, Jr., and the Laws that changed America. New York: Mariner Books, p.230. See also: http://www.tourismtoday.com/news/bahamas-pays-tribute-dr-martin-luther-king-jr [Retrieved: 4 September 2016].
[301] http://www.bahamas.com/resources/nassau-accord-1985 [Retrieved: 4 September 2016].

Made in United States
Troutdale, OR
12/30/2024